BUREAUCRACY
and
COMMUNITY

BUREAUCRACY
and
COMMUNITY

Essays on the Politics of Social Work Practice

**edited by
Linda Davies and Eric Shragge**

Montreal/New York

© BLACK ROSE BOOKS 1990

No part of this book may be reproduced or transmitted in any form by means, electronic or mechanical, including photocopying and recording, or by any information storage or retrieval, without written permission from the publisher, except for brief passages quoted by a reviewer in a newspaper or magazine.

BLACK ROSE BOOKS No. S146
Paperback ISBN: 0-921689-56-X
Hardcover ISBN: 0-921689-57-8

Canadian Cataloguing in Publication Data
Main entry under title:
Bureaucracy and Community

Includes bibliographical references.
ISBN 0-921689-57-8 (bound). --
ISBN 0-921689-56-X (pbk.)

1. Social service--Canada. 2. Social work administration--Canada. 3. Bureaucracy--Canada. I. Davies, Linda. II. Shragge, Eric, 1948-
HV31.B75 1990   361.971   C90-090137-3

Library of Congress Catalog No. 90-81638
Cover design: Pierre-Paul Pariseau
Design and Layout: Linda Barton

Editorial Offices
BLACK ROSE BOOKS
3981 St-Laurent Boulevard,
Suite 444
Montréal, Québec
H2W 1Y5 Canada

Mailing Address
BLACK ROSE BOOKS
P.O. Box 1258
Succ. Place du Parc
Montréal, Québec
H2W 2R3 Canada

U.S. Orders
BLACK ROSE BOOKS
340 Nagel Drive
Cheektowaga, New York
14225

Printed and bound in Québec, Canada
on acid-free paper

TABLE OF CONTENTS

Preface   7

Chapter One

Peter Leonard
FATALISM AND THE DISCOURSE ON POWER:
AN INTRODUCTORY ESSAY   9

Chapter Two

Wendy Thomson
MANAGING WHOSE PUBLIC SERVICES?   25

Chapter Three

Linda Davies
LIMITS OF BUREAUCRATIC CONTROL: SOCIAL WORKERS IN
CHILD WELFARE   81

Chapter Four

Laura Mastronardi
THE INUIT COMMUNITY WORKERS' EXPERIENCE OF YOUTH
PROTECTION WORK   103

Chapter Five

Eric Shragge
COMMUNITY BASED PRACTICE: POLITICAL ALTERNATIVES
OR NEW STATE FORMS?   137

BIBLIOGRAPHY   174

About The Authors

Linda Davies teaches at the School of Social Work, McGill University. She is the author of several articles on bureaucratic control and social work practice.

Peter Leonard teaches courses on social policy and administration, and on personality development and social structure at McGill University. He is currently working on a critical history of social work theories as forms of ideological transmission.

Laura Mastronardi has completed her MSW at the School of Social Work, McGill University. She has worked for many years in child welfare as a front line worker and a manager.

Eric Shragge teaches at the School of Social Work, McGill University. He has published in several areas including social policy, peace and disarmament, and community organization practice.

Wendy Thomson received her doctorate from Bristol University, England. She worked as a social worker in Montréal for many years and now holds a senior social service management position in London, England.

Preface

This volume introduces a new series of publications, jointly produced by the School of Social Work, McGill University and Black Rose Books, entitled ***Practice and Politics: McGill Studies***. The goals of this series are to bring—to the social worker and to the community—the issues and debates surrounding social work and social welfare; to publish, and to promote, the research and analysis that takes place in the School of Social Work at McGill; and to publish, and to promote, the material of other scholars and practicioners. In this endeavour, we gratefully acknowledge the financial support and the encouragement of the McGill School of Social Work Alumni Association.

This first volume, ***Bureaucracy and Community***, addresses current problems faced by social work practitioners working in both large bureaucracies and in community settings. Being trained as professionals, we internalize the belief that our practice should be autonomous, with decisions left to our own professional judgement. However, the relationship of our work places to the State, and the resulting labour processes, has, in recent years, overtaken and redefined our interventions in both state agencies and communities. This book will explore these central issues.

We wish to thank the following members of the Monograph Committee (School of Social Work, McGill): Jim Baumohl, Sydney Duder, Paul Cappon, Barbara Nichols, and, Peter Leonard, who contributed to the conception of this series and offered comments on the manuscripts submitted. In addition, all chapters were critically reviewed by outside readers. We thank: David Woodsworth, Nancy Guberman, Prue Rains and Jean Panet Raymond. Thanks also to Karen Chong-Kwan for typing, and Linda Barton of Black Rose Books for editorial assistance.

Chapter One

FATALISM AND THE DISCOURSE ON POWER: AN INTRODUCTORY ESSAY

Peter Leonard

When we speak of social work today many of us speak, it seems, in terms of increasing disillusionment. We experience a breaking of the illusion that we can act alongside those most impoverished, most oppressed, most hurt by our society. Instead of acting with, we act upon them; instead of being subjects, they are reduced to objects—categorized, classified, planned for, evaluated, monitored, reviewed. How can it be, we may say, that the commitment to social justice, the impulse to reach out to those most damaged by the social order, the will to act collectively to challenge those institutions which most oppress us all and which brought us into social work, have come to be subordinated to a technical practice from which these moral concerns seem to have been evacuated?

Disillusionment, however, does not describe all of the negative emotions which accompany many current discussions amongst social workers. Alongside the experience of a smashing of illusions is often an overwhelming sense of powerlessness. We may have lost some of our illusions, our beliefs even, but more significantly we feel quite unable to change the situations in which we find ourselves. We may detect ourselves acting upon our clients as if they were objects, but we experience a similar objectification of ourselves as social workers. When social workers are themselves treated as objects, the justification is couched in familiar of themselves as social workers. As the clients' desires and pains are re-formulated and categorized into 'needs', so are social workers' aspirations channelled into service for the organization.

The last step in the downward spiral from earlier aspirations experienced by many social workers is not usually named openly in discussion, for it seems to contradict the cultural expectations of the bourgeois professional in their daily life, with its apparent opportunity to make choices, to change things. I am speaking here of fatalism, of resignation in the face of that which oppresses and controls us. We have tried to resist, but we have failed and now we are stuck. It is hard to be optimistic, easier to express hopelessness in the face of an accumulation of experiences of defeat. Paulo Freire (1970) has shown us that the fatalism of Brazilian peasants can be confronted with the development of a critical consciousness which shows such fatalism as culturally constructed to serve the dominant order of things. Perhaps we, also, should see our tendency to fatalism as internalized ideology?

Do I paint too bleak a picture? I think not. Not only are these feelings of disillusionment, powerlessness and fatalism strongly held by many social workers in Canada, they have their parallels in the experiences of social workers in other countries where a 'welfare State' structure of public services provides the location for most social work practice. In this volume, there is empirical material on both Québec and Britain, and to these examples could be added reflections on my own intensive contact with social workers in Denmark, Norway, Sweden and Australia. These contacts all speak to the same depressing discourse.

To speak of social workers' feelings is not to psychologize away their powerlessness; much of this volume can be used to explain the objective, structural origins of these feelings. To speak of feelings is to acknowledge the significance of the internalization of material circumstances and the role of ideology in constructing both our perceptions of those circumstances and the possibility, or impossibility, of changing them.

In the discourse on power and powerlessness, social workers turn their attention to the State, and in particular to state bureaucratic structures as constituting their most immediate material circumstances as social workers. Those who make the subsequent contributions to this book—Linda Davies, Laura Mastronardi, Eric Shragge, and Wendy Thomson—confront the problem of state bureaucracies as a vehicle for social service provision, the relation between state power and democratic processes, and the possibilities of community involvement and control of services. Attitudes to the State as revealed in these essays range from a belief in the progressive possibilities of state power as part of a political struggle, to outright hostility to the State as manifesting, inevitably, the domination of centralized structures representing class, gender, and ethnic oppression. At the centre of this book is a debate. It is a dispute about the State and its progressive possibilities. This argument is of critical significance to the daily experience of social workers especially those who are employed as agents of the State. Although they carry the authority of the State and have some opportunities for manoeuvre and avoidance, they feel, and are, relatively powerless as individuals. What are the options available to them? Is it to be progressive social workers or progressive managers within the State apparatus of social services? Is it to commitment to, and support for, a growth of alternative community-based services and their accompanying political struggles? Are these options mutually exclusive? Are social workers to respond positively to their powerlessness and counteract their fatalism through struggle in the State, against the State, or 'in and against' the State?

All of the essays which follow provide the empirical support of research findings to argue their respective positions, within the left, on issues of practice and theory. The purpose of this introductory essay is to follow through to the origins of social workers' often negative experience of their practice and its context, and in so doing, to relate to each other the subsequent contributions. To undertake this task I shall focus on three issues: the crisis in state welfare; theory about the State; and the nature of the debate on state welfare and its implications for social work practice.

Crisis

Within the tradition of left critique, we might say that state health and social services in capitalist countries are always in a condition of crisis. It is a crisis resulting from the fundamental contradiction encountered by the State when attempting to finance services and benefits and, at the same time, maintain, reproduce and strengthen an economy built upon the necessity for capital accumulation and profitability. Even though, as both Davies and Thomson argue, the relative autonomy of the State enables it to be subject to the struggle of different political forces, nevertheless, the imperatives of a capitalist economy, now of international dimensions, are always, I believe, decisive in the last resort.

When economies are in boom, as they were from the post-war period until the mid-seventies throughout the advanced capitalist world, then state services can be financed by social democratic or liberal governments without seriously affecting the rate of accumulation and profitability. The contradiction, in other words, can be managed provided services remain as a modest proportion of the national product. In times of general recession, of changes in the forces of production, or of the relocation of investment capital in the search for lowest labour costs and highest profits, state services are often the first to suffer.

For at least a decade and a half, social work within western capitalist countries has been practiced in a context of cuts and restructuring. Crisis has been experienced as endemic, first at the level of resources and later also at the level of ideology. Whilst, in Thomson's phrase, "the social democratic spell" still lingers within the organizations of state welfare, the neo-conservative challenge and its present hegemony has profoundly shifted the ideological parameters of mainstream debate about the possibilities and limits of state provision (see Leonard 1990). Social workers are now attempting to deliver social services during a period of historic retreat from the notion of a universal, comprehensive welfare State, a notion which was established in most western countries after the Second World War. This social democratic/liberal welfare State proved not to be the democratic and participative vehicle for progressive social change that many of us had hoped. Its remote, bureaucratic and controlling features made it especially vulnerable to attack from the radical right with its rhetorical emphasis on freedom from state interference and the supposed choice which is provided by the market. Because the neo-conservatives see the recipients of state benefits as a burden on the "productive sector", their "burden theory of welfare" (Phillipson and Walker 1986) inserts itself increasingly into common sense, into general discourse about social services especially those aimed at the most vulnerable sectors of the population who are least able to defend themselves.

For social workers this crisis of welfare is, then, ideological as much as it is a crisis of resources. As conceptions of social welfare have changed, both social workers and service users have experienced increasing alienation. The State, seen once as a vehicle of participative, democratic change, is now seen as malignant rather than benign, as that which treats us as objects, an enterprise in which it is not possible to have any faith. The neo-conservative political project, even when the agency at the local level has a degree of relative autonomy from central government, has the effect, Thomson shows us, of gradually transforming the relationship between the political leaders and the social service managers. To struggle against neo-conservative ideology, to hold to the remnants of a social democratic vision is a hard road, even for senior bureaucrats, when their authority is newly under political attack from the right, as well as, more traditionally, from the left.

The crisis through which we are living can be understood, then, as constructed by both left and right. The old social democratic institutions, once the source of hope, came to be subjected to severe criticism from the left for their sexism and racism and for their remote bureaucratic structures. But these left critics, however, have been forced, when faced with conservative attacks, to turn around and defend these very same structures from the cost-cutting and dismantling which is the material effect of neo-conservative ideology. What is the left to do now? Shragge argues that it should look at alternatives to the State as a vehicle for social services, something which it has given too little attention to. "The crisis of the welfare State", he maintains, "should have provided an opportunity, both in theory and practice, for the left to propose concrete options that were neither in the statist tradition of the centre/left, nor (of)...the right..." Faith in state solutions was in any case misplaced from the start, perhaps, and disillusionment inevitable. Given the empirical evidence provided by Mastronardi on the impact of state power on Inuit community workers and their subordination to it, we can appreciate the strength of the argument against service provision within the state apparatus, especially where it is based so evidently on institutional racism. I shall return to this argument later. What we can mark now is that the current material and ideological crisis over the provision of social services involves conflict about the role of state power in relation to community participation and control.

Theory

In criticizing the left for having failed to respond effectively to neo-conservative attacks on the welfare State, Shragge points to its general lack of a commitment to non-State alternatives. He points to a failure in theory as well as practice. But beneath this statement about failure, and underlying the debate about the State and bureaucracy, is something as yet unsaid. All of the authors of this book situate themselves on the left of politics, and all draw upon, to varying degrees, Marxist categories of analysis: State, class, economy, power, ideology, and other central concepts understood within the Marxist tradition. What lies beneath this theoretical discourse is the fact that Marxism itself is part of the crisis—that it faces the question of whether it is now obsolete as a basis for critique. Eastern Europe seems to be answering this question with a resounding 'yes' and, in so doing, suggesting perhaps that for the West also it is not possible to have a critical theory of society which ties itself to the Marxist tradition. This is not, of course, an abstract 'academic' question, because if social workers are not to draw on Marxism for critique, where are they to turn? On what basis of social theory are they to struggle to develop a critical practice? For many of us, even feminism, powerful as it is, cannot yet stand on its own, but needs the analysis of class, of production, of capitalism, to stand alongside the analysis of patriarchy.

Perhaps, in clinging still to Marxism, we avoid confronting a challenge which is issued to all those who attempt to build structures and organizations—State or non-State—with the intention of 'helping people', namely, that the structures are forever doomed also to control people. Perhaps the sense of fatalism which social workers experience when they try to think how they might attempt to change bureaucratic structures to reflect the clients' interests is not, after all, internalized defeatist ideology, but rather the result of a realistic assessment. Before we comment on the debate about the State and its alternatives, we must face this possibility and argue it through.

Anti-Humanism

In a sustained, critical attack on all existing ideologies of social work, Rojek, Peacock and Collins argue against the humanism which underlies them all. "Humanism", they suggest, "is primarily a philosophy of action. It maintains that human beings, in pursuit of their own willed ends, 'make their own history'. Such thought places human beings at the centre of the world. It assumes that 'we' basically have the same problems" (*op. cit.* 1988: 114). In traditional social work, these humanist assumptions lead to workers seeing themselves as helpers and carers, and clients as having essentially the same properties of 'consciousness', 'reason', 'responsibility', and 'choice'. Because of a belief in the existence of common human needs, social workers and their clients experience "the paradoxical nature of humanist caring". In deciding and categorizing the 'needs' of people the process of monitoring, judging, evaluating and assessing take place. In 'helping', social work also controls. The clients' desires are transformed, through procedures of professional assessment, into 'needs' which fit into the pre-formed categories learned during training and refined and reinforced in agency manuals and protocols. Thomson provides a striking example of this process in her description of the relationship between social service managers and agency clients, a description which is worthy of Foucault:

> Most of the relations with clients goes on in the managers' heads in categories that have assumed professional meaning, the elements of people's experience that defines them for the institution—the six client group categories of children and families, under fives, elderly, mentally ill, mentally handicapped, physically handicapped. These are the categories in which the community is discussed at management meetings and in policy debate…'Client groups' in turn grow into 'bodies of professional knowledge' or specialisms which have to be protected if the needs of those groups are to be properly met.

Although both Davies and Mastronardi argue that bureaucratic control over social work practice has its *limits*, we, nevertheless, are to understand from their work that it is a control which is omnipresent as a tendency, central to the social services management of human 'needs' and human 'problems'. The social workers studied by Davies are, in any case, highly ambivalent about this organizational control: they have come to fear not the control, but their own autonomy and discretion, and look to control as a means of managing their uncertainty. But subordination to bureaucratic control is, Mastronardi shows us, even more marked where that control is "white man's law", and where the low professional identity of the Inuit community workers, and their role conflict, within their communities, leads them to despondency and passive subordination.

The managers and practitioners studied by Davies, Mastronardi, and Thomson are not identified as especially 'radical'; they are within the mainstream in attempting to deliver a service which is permeated with control and regulation. "Inuit", Mastronardi tells us, "are socialized to a tradition of undifferentiated helping, whereas professional helping is grounded in a functional division of labour." This division of labour, these "bodies of professional knowledge" are the basic structures of social work as an occupation and a practice. They are structures of discourse and regulation which play their part in the establishment, in contemporary society, of forms of social management which have moved from the direct repression and punishment of deviants to their care, discipline and "humane" control. Foucault characterizes our role in ensuring that people act in officially approved ways, thus:

> We are in the society of the teacher-judge, the doctor-judge, the educator-judge, the 'social worker'-judge; it is on them that the universal reign of the normative is based; and each individual, wherever he may find himself, subjects to it his body, his gestures, his behaviour, his aptitudes, his achievements (Foucault 1975: 304).

These characteristics of traditional, mainstream social work have been subjected also to the critique of Marxism and feminism, though in a language appropriate to a different discourse on the political and the personal. Does this mean, we may hope, that 'radical' social workers, or 'progressive' social services managers, effectively void this attempt at normative control over those with whom they work? But we already know the answer even while we are asking the question. Surely, it is *no*. Is the attempted exercise of normative control the exclusive domain of the State apparatus, or can we see it as permeating all forms of practice, including those which take place within community-based alternative organizations?

Unfortunately, the argument against humanism can be used effectively against humanist forms of radical or critical social work practice. Marxist and feminist social workers, like conservatives, believe that people have common needs, that they can be either repressed or liberated, and radicals believe that social change can take place through collective, transformative action. But the condition of post-modern society, argue Rojek, Peacock, and Collins, is one of paradox, uncertainty, suspense, difference.

> Modernism refers to the type of social consciousness which is characteristic of modern societies: a form of social consciousness which views itself and the world as dynamic, many-sided, fragmentary, and discontinuous. Modernization increases the velocity of life; it challenges traditional order and religion; through science it shatters and dissolves all firmly held belief...(*op. cit.* 1988: 161).

In such a society, the authors suggest, the attempt at normative control is increasingly fraught with difficulty, just as is the attempt to mobilize collectively. In modern society, the very concept of community is essentially a nostalgic one, a romantic, impossible idea. The language we use when we talk of needs, of solidarity, or of collectivity no longer have a meaning which connects to the reality of how we feel and how we live in modern society, fragmented and isolated. The crisis of modern society is also a crisis of language, and the discourse of social work, both radical and conservative, performs the function of mystifying the uncertainty, paradox, mistrust and degradation of everyday life. It creates the illusion that effective action, from the right or from the left, can be undertaken to alleviate pain and suffering—a comforting belief in a world of uncertainty.

Stated in their most brutal form, these arguments against humanism, these emphases on the repressive functions of discourse, these characterizations of post-modern society, all combine to seem to render authentic the experiences of powerlessness, disillusion and fatalism which we have identified as part of the crisis in contemporary social work. But what are we to make of this depressing, relativist analysis? Can we use the powerful critique embedded in these perspectives without abandoning a critical social theory still linked to Marxism and feminism, still committed to collective change? Can we draw upon these penetrating examinations of post-modern society, the emphases on the analysis of discourse, the demystifications of the paradox of care and control, and use them to understand the nature of the debate about the State and about community alternatives to state provision?

When we reach, in this essay, the point at which it is necessary to comment on the central debate in this book, a tentative attempt will have been made to answer this latter question. But first, we must consider whether Marxist analysis still has a function to perform for us, and so we must do a little more theoretical work.

Peter Leonard

Marxist Discourse

I have suggested that the problem of Marxism is part of the current crisis within radical, critical social work. Because Marxism has come to be perceived as profoundly problematic, the left, including as it is, however poorly, represented in social work, finds itself with nowhere to turn. Can we be confident in the Marxist categories of analysis that we try to use in debating the State and its alternatives as the location for social welfare?

In writing about the intellectual role of Habermas in the development of critical theory, Roderick (1986) shows us that critical theory is an emancipatory project based on the assumption that history can be made by "will and consciousness"—a humanist program *par excellence*. But most interestingly in the context of our present discussion, we can note the fact that Habermas sees the future of critical theory as one which remains in the Marxist tradition but which at the same time takes a "linguistic turn"—concerns itself with language and communication.

In classical Marxism, the paradigm of production is the basis for the understanding of human life. Human experiences are shared, are common, because they are constituted historically as a result of productive activity—the application of labour to nature. The irrationalities of this productive activity, of people's immediate material existence, can only be transformed by the working class through social struggle. But this classical model has effectively collapsed. It has collapsed because, according to Habermas (see Roderick 1986: 155), the working class seems to have lost its revolutionary potential and become totally incorporated into the structures and ideologies of capitalism. At the same time, capitalism no longer legitimates itself primarily by reference to social norms and values. Freedom, the common good, equality of opportunity, are words in a discourse which have lost their meaning. Rather, capitalism's legitimation comes from the promise and delivery of a technologically secured rise in material standards. In the words of Rojek, Peacock and Collins, contemporary capitalism is a post-modern society where "through the money economy and the commercialization of products and experience it reduces all value to cash value"(*op. cit.*1988: 161).

Do these historical developments in capitalism, the alleged decomposition of the paradigm of production and the incorporation of the working class, spell the end of Marxism as an emancipatory analysis and politics? Certainly, there are strong arguments from Foucault and others concerned with communication and discourse that Marxism is, at the very least, an obsolete mode of discourse. Beaurillard, in his theoretical and radical political opposition to Marxism (see Roderick 1986: 152-154), argues that Marxism is, in fact, part of the structures of repression. Marxism's discourse on production and its view of human beings as workers are part of the degradation and distortion of contemporary society. Rather than focus on production, Beaurillard contends, we should analyze the repressive discourse of capitalism whereby the "needs" generated by production are totally false: "Needs lose all their autonomy; they are coded" (Roderick *op. cit.*: 153). This "terrorism of the code", the discourse of capitalism, makes it impossible for us, either as the working class or as the professional and intellectual strata, as social workers, to engage in the profound critique and action which is necessary for social transformation. This is because "whatever one does, one can only respond to the system in its own terms, according to its own rules, answering it with its own signs" (Roderick *op. cit.*: 153).

What are the practice implications of this argument? Surely, it is not logical to accept that the dominant, repressive discourse is so total that attacks on this discourse are rendered impossible? If this were the case, then Beaurillard and other radical discourse theorists would themselves have been unable to make *their* critique. More usefully, discourse theory turns our attention to the problematic nature of communication and meaning and encourages us to take a "linguistic turn" in our own analysis of social work practice within the State apparatus and within community organizations. Whilst we might agree that the "terrorism of the code" tends to subordinate the major classes, bourgeoisie and proletariat, to a dominant discourse which encloses their conceptions of the social world, we might also turn our attention to that part of the population with whom social workers are most in contact, the so-called "third sector"—those living on the margin in poverty and unemployment, single parents, native Indian people, oppressed black populations, young people without any hope for their futures. Beaurillard suggests that there is a population "outside the code" of women, youth, students, black people and elderly people who are "relegated to a position of non-place of the code" (Roderick *op. cit.*: 154). This is a group outside society, not really addressed by the discourse and therefore one might suggest able to understand itself in terms other than those required of the dominant code. This is not the organized white male proletariat which was to be the transformative force of classical Marxism, but a substantial segment of the oppressed population as yet relatively unorganized. (Twenty-four percent of the population of Montréal live below the poverty line, according to Statistics Canada.)

When we think of this third sector we must be careful not to indulge in romantic fantasies about their revolutionary role. The discourse of the left has in the past been saturated with a rhetoric about the revolutionary and emancipatory potential of the working class in advanced capitalist countries, a discourse about "the vanguard", about "liberation", about "struggle", which has served to mystify the realities of radical politics. Nevertheless, the third sector are those with whom we are likely to work most frequently, both in community organizations and as users of state services. To what extent can radical social workers assist in the process of mobilizing this population, especially within their communities, challenging the "terror of the code" and, with them, confronting dominant definitions of their situations and the policies and practices which flow from these definitions?

In modern societies, the State apparatus occupies a dominant role in the manufacture of the oppressive discourse which categorizes, defines, and ultimately judges and disciplines us. How monolithic is that apparatus, and how open to challenge is the discourse which it fosters? It seems to me that in the debate about the State and about community alternatives as arenas for progressive social developments, these questions are crucial. To begin to answer them a Marxist analysis remains, I believe, essential, but only if it is interrogated and ultimately transformed by an understanding of social divisions which no longer prioritizes class, but sees it as a critical structural dynamic alongside gender, race and other divisions which distribute economic, social, cultural and psychological benefits. Marxism must also take its "linguistic turn", understanding and confronting dominant discourses and examining its own.

Debate

And so we come, finally, to the debate. How are we to characterize it? In what language can we render an account of its elements and the various levels at which it takes place? It is not the purpose of this last section of the essay to summarize the arguments put forward, or to resolve them and formulate some concluding consensus. The reader will, no doubt, take sides, see some arguments as more convincing than others, accept some analyses and reject others. My aim here is to provide a commentary of questions and discussion which may throw some light on the nature of this discourse within the left.

At the start of this essay, I addressed the crisis which many social workers experience, not in the language of academic theory, but in the language of feelings. These feelings, of disillusionment, of powerlessness, of fatalism, are, we can see, socially constructed within the material and ideological experiences of their work and of their daily lives. As we approach the academic discourse about the State and its community alternatives, we may see beneath it another discourse, one similarly of emotions and equally constructed within the material and ideological experiences of the authors. On the surface the authors are, in this book, addressing similar objects, but at the same time their emphases are different, and their specialisms, the division of academic labour—management, child welfare, community organization—lead them in different directions. Beneath the academic discourse there surfaces at times the emotions generated by interests, beliefs and experiences, though usually expressed in the language of theoretical analysis and empirical observation and description. All of us in this book reveal our optimism and pessimism, our hope and despair. Hostility towards the state apparatus links to a belief in the possibility of alternatives. Working within the State, as all of us do who write this book, may lead us to feel compelled to justify the location of our work with a belief in the possibilities of acting, to some degree, *against* the State.

To relate emotions to interests and beliefs is not to psychologize away the objective forces which construct these emotions: rather, I have suggested that it enables us to understand more fully how we engage in a particular discourse and how the discourse shapes us. This is a discourse within the left, and so we use the particular language generated within that discourse, and especially the words consecrated by Marxism. What meanings do these words now hold for us, the writers, and for you, the readers?

When we speak about the State, what image arises in our minds? For some, it is best represented by Kafka, a menacing and controlling entity, a monolith which crushes us and subordinates us to the "terror of the code". For others, it is shot through with contradictions, it is at times messily inchoate and it simply cannot control us as much as its politicians and bureaucrats would wish. In the one image, the state agent is trapped for a lifetime in the dominant discourse, speaking forever in the unauthentic and increasingly meaningless language of specialized knowledge, of client categories, of interventive strategies, of community planning. In another image, we see the state worker as hero, doing battle against bureaucratic structures, making alliances with community groups, linking up with social movements, and suffering burnout.

When we speak about the community, what images arise for us then? Do we get that warm feeling which comes from a picture of solidarity, of collectivity in the face of adversity, of the shared humour of those who have so little to laugh at? Or do we, on the other hand, picture the conflict and the competition, the sexism and racism of people's relationships and the struggles for power? For any of these images, empirical evidence might be offered for support, but it is the dominant images which will do much to shape our response to the state provision of social services and the possibilities of community-based alternatives.

Whether state agents, either social workers or social service managers, can act effectively to resist the bureaucratic power of which they are part, are forced, as Thomson suggests, to "take sides" as members of the new petit bourgeoisie, depends upon how power is seen as distributed. Althusser (1971) with his theory of 'State Ideological Apparatuses' sees power as highly concentrated, and in consequence sees state workers, like all workers, submerged, passively, beneath the terrible weight of the apparatus; political struggle is given little attention because it is generally futile. On the other hand, Foucault (1980) sees power as more diffused, as generated in many locations within society; it is manifested in a discourse in which the language of 'needs', the language of 'the expert', is a form of control which constructs our understandings of ourselves and our social world. At the same time, Foucault, like many discourse theorists, sees collective action as ultimately generating new forms of oppression in the interests of a new 'radical' discourse.

To argue for either struggles within the State, or against the State from outside, from community organizations, requires a voluntarist, non-determinist philosophy. Power cannot be conceived as so centralized and monolithic that resistance is impossible. Discourse analysis helps us to see how diffused it is, but for me voluntarism, a belief in the efficacy of human intention in producing change rather than the blind forces of history, leads me to reject the idea that collective action will inevitably result in new forms of oppression. The dominant discourses of care and control can be challenged both within the State apparatus and from outside it. Challenging the hegemonic codes effectively requires collectivity and not simply individual refusal, however heroic that may seem. Collectivity is necessary in order to attempt to establish pre-figurative relationships, relationships which try to confront the sexism, racism and control in our own discourses, whether we work within the State or in community groups.

This book lies with a left social work discourse about the State, about power and about the community. All of the authors in the essays which follow speak of the great problems and difficulties to be faced in the work they describe: the conflicts experienced by the Inuit community worker faced with the white man's law; the fears and uncertainties of child protection workers; the dilemmas of managers standing between neo-conservative politicians and service users; the issues of compromise and co-operation with the State faced by community organizations. All of these problems might lead one to feel overwhelmed, but the authors remain cautiously optimistic that change is possible and that resistance can be mounted. Fatalism is not a necessary element in the discourse on social work, the State and the community.

Chapter Two

MANAGING WHOSE PUBLIC SERVICES?[1]

Wendy Thomson

In England and in Canada, we are emerging from a period where public services have been under attack: most obviously in terms of public expenditure, but also in terms of public confidence. To move, in a progressive way, from this position of unpopularity from without and uncertainty from within, will mean taking a hard look at some of our ideas and experiences of social service organization and accountability. Managers will have to play a part in that re-examination, and they may not get a second chance.

For social service organizations to move forward means constructing a practice which not only connects with social concerns, but which is also organized in an efficient way. Both elements are essential so that public services continue to exist into the 1990s, and they are so for three main reasons: to convince working class people that there is an alternative to the narrow financial efficiency of accountants, that 'public' is not synonymous with sloppy and expensive; to persuade people, through the only real way that people do learn things, that the public sector can work, by experiencing public organizations that *do* work well; and, to demonstrate that social concern is not a misplaced old-fashioned idea that has had to be sacrificed on the altar of personal success/failure and material consumption, but integral to the life people want for each other and themselves. Personal and social welfare may again become connected in the nineties as the effects of their separation develop.

There is considerable evidence that people do not experience the public sector as working in the way that it should. Working class people need to feel that it works for *them*. My experience as a manager and researcher in public services convinces me that these are not institutions that are delivering change— for anybody. In the past, social services may have experienced themselves as more competent. Organizations may have seemed less chaotic, staff may have been happier, clients may have received more benevolent attention, but currently there is little evidence that the services are working responsively in the interests of the public.

An element of progressive management will involve constructing ways of demonstrating the effectiveness of social service organizations. In the longer term, some might wish to demonstrate the effectiveness of a more radical organization, but in this period, which can hardly be characterized as one of socialist transformation in most western democracies, the most that can be done from within state management is to construct the conditions where a progressive practice might exist. In order to move forward, or perhaps even to exist, public organizations have to develop a meaningful relationship to the public. Managers of public service organizations will have to be involved in constructing that relationship.

From my experience of management and research I believe that any management theory which seeks to inform practice must be drawn from an analysis of managers' experience. The study of social service managers on which this essay is based was undertaken in England and Québec in the mid-eighties. The study analyzed managers' experience of change during that period, the structures in which they worked and their role within those structures.

Experience, as expressed through personal interview, is seldom a type of evidence used in management research. It is also uncommon to rely on qualitative data in an international study, but this approach overcomes many of the criticisms commonly levelled against comparative studies which are based upon statistical evidence collected at a national level. Managers' accounts alone no more convey a total reality than does statistical evidence, but it is a reality of some importance.

However, the methodology consisted not only of interviews with managers, but recognized the interaction of theory, history and social structure in producing analysis. Accounts of managers alone, or the history of social agencies, or contemporary political economy each contributes to our understanding of the limits and possibilities of social service management. That understanding is enriched by the interaction of methods. Drawing upon data in two countries, without undertaking a comparative empirical study, also moved the analysis away from the common sense assumptions and explanations that descriptive case studies sometimes reproduce.

Although there is no particular rationale for choosing the two organizations involved in this study—one in Devon (England) and the other in Montréal (Québec)—I did have access, both physically and culturally, to both organizations through my time in England and background in Québec. To be able to relate to managers with an appreciation of their position is, I believe, as important to the analysis of interview material as computer and statistical skills are to quantitative material.

The fieldwork of this research was undertaken in 1983 and 1984 and involved in-depth structured interviews with forty-two managers (twenty-four in Montréal at Ville Marie Social Service Centre; and eighteen in Devon Social Service Department in Devon County Council). In addition, I interviewed fifteen individuals who were either clients, members of the Board of Directors, social work staff, or trade union officials. The fieldwork included: examination of minutes of departmental decision-making bodies (i.e., Board of Directors [Ville Marie], Social Service Committee of elected Members [Devon County Council], senior management teams, area management teams); government directives; and organizational documents (i.e., charts, forward planning statements, financial statements).

All forty-two management interviews were tape-recorded and transcribed in full, then subjected to analysis in terms of themes and concepts informed by relevant theoretical and historical work. In accordance with the 'multi-method' described above, it is necessary to locate both agencies and service systems in an historical context. The complete research report contains a detailed consideration of the political economy of England and Québec in the mid-eighties, and an historical account of the 'social production' of social service managers brought into existence by government commissions (Thomson 1988).

One of the interesting facts which allowed a study of social service organization in England and Québec is that the forms of both institutions were established as a result of government commissions in the late sixties: the Seebohm Commission in England, and the Castonguay-Nepveu Commission in Québec. The statutory duties inscribed in the social service institutions created, as a result of the work of these two Commissions, are broadly similar: child protection; services to families and children; the elderly; people with physical and learning disabilities; and problems of mental health.

The main difference is that the Québec Social Service Centre (Ville Marie SSC) is part of a wider health and social service network (*réseau*) coordinated at a regional level but accountable provincially to the Ministry of Social Affairs of the Government of Québec. The English Social Service Department (Devon SSD) is a local authority department and is directed by the County Council and its Councillors who are politically elected members. Both organizations have an Area structure, but Ville Marie provides primarily a fieldwork service, whereas Devon SSD also manages day care and residential provision.

Ville Marie had a total staff of six hundred and eighteen in 1982, serving an English-speaking population of four hundred twenty thousand (Ministry of Social Affairs, 1982).[2] Devon SSD had a staff of three thousand, four hundred and eighty-seven in 1982, of which four hundred and forty-five were fieldworkers, and one hundred and fifty-five were Administrators and managers, and serves a population of nine hundred forty-eight thousand (Devon Population estimates 1981). Ville Marie's budget was twenty-two million dollars in 1982/83, and Devon's was twenty-seven million pounds sterling. Radically different wage levels and fluctuating exchange rates make any direct budgetary comparisons between these two organizations meaningless.

One practical problem with international study involving local qualitative data is the vast amount of descriptive detail necessary for readers to fully understand local and organizational references contained in managers' accounts. An article of this length is difficult to pitch at the right level of detail, and to offer instrumental help, a glossary of abbreviations, with Québec terms in French and English, is provided at the end of this essay. The argument put forward here does not rely upon detailed empirical knowledge of the settings of these two organizations, but rather focusses on the relations these managers experience with the public.

I have outlined a direction for social service management to move as it enters the 1990s. However, the possibility for progressive management practice can only exist if it is possible to effect change from within state institutions. Simply, can anything be done? And, can professional managers have a part in doing it?

This is a central and nagging concern for many working in state management at the moment, as well as for politicians for whom they work. The suspicion that nothing can be done from within the State no doubt plays a part in leading progressive professionals to seek employment elsewhere. It is a question which lies at the heart of the uncertainty and alienation felt by many of those working for state social services, and therefore affects those trying to decide whether or not to work in such agencies, or those teaching, those working or thinking about working, in the State. In a social service world where service users had a say, no doubt they too would be concerned about the future of public services.

Professions and State Organizations

In the sixties' and seventies' expansion of state employment and provision in public services, the social service profession's main worry focused on the threat of bureaucratization and state takeover. Later, as these same sectors faced expenditure cuts and wavering political support, professional concern shifted to its survival. It became clear, at least to some, that worse things could happen to a profession than being bureaucratized: it could cease to exist at all.

Ceasing to exist has been on the agenda for social work teaching and practice over the last decade in some western democracies. Whatever individual decisions social workers may make about working in the State or not, there is little doubt that the nature of social work's professional future is tied to the future of state supported social services. These institutions can survive without the social work profession, but as the reverse is not the case, examining the possibilities for constructing a future for these institutions should be a key professional concern.

In important respects, the question 'what can be done?' is about power; the question of 'what can be done working within the State?' is about state power. Too many accounts of management start and end with the managers themselves, placing them at the centre of state bureaucratic processes as the most powerful force. Although I would agree that man-agers are potentially an important group, they are neither as powerful as some bourgeois and critical writing suggests nor as powerless as they often feel. To pursue the reality of a progressive state management practice means understanding the possibilities and limits of that power, its limits and possibilities which relate to democratic forces, and professionals' accountability to them.

Theories of State Managers

Theory has a role to play in informing management research and practice, but to be useful it must allow for the possibility of agency within the State. It cannot assume that nothing can be done due to the overriding determinism of state structures, yet a great deal of theory does just that. Equally, theory which assumes an unconstrained agency, as so much management theory does, will not help in analyzing the structured world which managers must play a part in managing. Managers need to be considered theoretically, in terms of their location within state organizations, and also in terms of their social relations outside the State in civil society.

My study of managers was constructed primarily in relation to non-determinist Marxist approaches to the State; nevertheless, it is also important to understand some of the themes contained within another approach to the State, that of social democracy. Used as a political theory, social democracy offers an understanding of the history of the British or Québec States that has been not only an intellectually critical theory, but has played a role in the construction of practice itself. In an important sense, aspects of social democracy have been incorporated into the practice and thoughts about practice that are a part of the institutions where these managers work. However, such a theory can never adequately provide an analytic perspective to the object of study.

Nonetheless, one of the main theories of social policy in Britain has been constructed almost totally within the boundaries of social democratic political theory—social administration. This discipline exists as one of the major ways in which welfare State activity in general and the activities of managers in particular are researched and understood in universities, in Britain and to a lesser extent in Canada. In the nineties it is questionable that social administration has much direct impact on the actual practice of welfare institutions. But moving away from practice to the debates about ideas that take place in universities, social administration forms a part of the intellectual support to social service institutions and professionals. Social administration thus provides some of the intellectual framework which influences how managers actually understand what they do, where they work, and the nature of the power that they have.

What role does the public play in the way social administration theory understands change? The main focus of much social administrative research and writing is on the institutions through which any change will occur. It assumes that social change will come about mainly through the agency of the State and the State will be primarily changed through the medium of legislation. It should be stressed that this is, in historical terms, a very minor part of the way in which social change is actually brought about. But in social administrative theory, legislation is paramount and Parliament not only 'creates legislation' but also 'has power'. The majority party wins power over Parliament through winning elections.

Most politics takes place in a limited way: the people vote, Parliament is elected, and the process of change is one of implementation. Implementation, however, is left to professionals and experts outside the political process. This attitude to politics reveals what is a largely unstated theory of the State which underlies social democratic practice and social administrative research. It assumes that both policy and change are neutral administrative activities, that in order to be effective each must be free of political interference. Policy is to be implemented based on scientific rationality and technique. 'Policy failure' is regarded as a malfunction requiring technical adjustment. Institutions are either functional—meeting the demands of the next period of development—or they are replaced by new ones. Empirical evaluations of the effectiveness of state institutions—the facts—serve to demonstrate the functionality of structures in implementing policy aims. For social administrative research, the facts take on far greater importance in changing the world than people do.

I have outlined the two main obstacles—people and politics—to the rational development of change to which social administration is devoted. If only they could be kept out of it so much would be possible, or so goes the social democratic plea. However, as the gap is realized between stated aims and expectations of welfare policy and its actual achievements, the main explanation and prescriptions in the U.K. have been provided by Thatcherism. Ironically, it may now be easier to suggest that the gap between aim and effect, between the idea and material reality, not only needs explanation, but may be beyond the explanatory power of what passes for social administrative theory.

Social administration's stress upon resources, on electoral politics and positivistic facts combines to produce an ideology of management that acts as a siphon, cut off from politics and political relationships. As we shall see, these lessons taught by social democracy—lessons of managerial distance from the people and politics—have taken their toll.

By contrast, Marxist theories provide a perspective which is both outside social democracy but which shares with it an interest in change involving the State. Within Marxist theories, the personnel of the State raise theoretical questions which cut across two major areas: changes in the class structure, particularly the location of those who work in the expanding service sector; and the emergence of the welfare State. It is Poulantzas' (1978) concept of relative autonomy that marks a significant departure in the debate about the State. This concept, and his subsequent treatment of classes and state personnel suggest ways of understanding the position and practice of state managers that lie outside social democratic thinking.

For Poulantzas, state personnel are conceived in two ways. First, the 'bureaucracy' is defined in terms of a specific social category as a group which derives a unity from its relationship to the institutions of the State. Second, state personnel are defined in terms of their class affiliation which is derived from their position in the social, rather than technical, division of labour, most importantly their decisionary role in the organization of politics and ideology.

Within this formulation, whilst there is recognition that those working in the State share an experience which permits them to be considered a group, they cannot be above or separate from classes. There cannot be a class of 'bureaucrats' who are determined by, and derive a power from, the State's power which they can then use to further their own interests: the processes by which state bureaucracy and the classes within it operate are seen to be more complex and need to be understood in their relation to the balance of forces within and outside the State.

There is not one class within the State but three in Poulantzas' analysis, and the majority of middle managers he assigns to the new petit bourgeoisie (NPB), not because the class acts as a conduit within the State for the bourgeois domination of the working class, but rather because it forms within itself a 'living example' of the internalized functioning of these relations. The NPB is characterized by the fact that its agents exercise over others political relations reflecting in the image, albeit a distorted one, of society's overall social relations. Through bureaucratization NPB agents are not only subordinate to the management above, but reproduce these features within their internal class relations. "Each bureaucratized instance both subordinates and is subordinated" (Poulantzas 1978: 275).

There are important consequences of Poulantzas' assigning the middle and lower levels of state institutions to the NPB, for a class outside the dominant capitalist relations of production, polarized between the bourgeoisie and the proletariat, cannot operate autonomously to serve its own interests. It must necessarily depend on either the bourgeoisie or the proletariat to improve or maintain its position. In the long run to have any effect it must take sides.

This is quite a different consequence from that suggested by theories of the 'middle class'. Such theories are in agreement that there is a distinct group between the two major classes, but in contrast to Poulantzas it is represented as a group possessing certain sets of occupations, levels of income, lifestyles, etc. The middle class group so defined is then considered the dominant class in society by virtue of its numerical dominance. According to these formulations of the middle class, those working within the State acquire a power both from their membership in an expanding middle group in society at large, and from their membership in an all-powerful bureaucracy.

Poulantzas argues the reverse: the capacity of the NPB to organize themselves as an effective political force is limited. The effect of the NPB presence within the State (i.e., its antagonism to the bourgeoisie as well as internal divisions within the bourgeoisie and its fractions), is manifested in the many breaks and dislocations that occur within and between different state branches, departments and levels. These breaks and conflicts are not seen as 'dysfunctional' or abnormal as they are in theories of bureaucracy, but form the contradictions which are the very stuff of the State and the opportunities for its transformation.

Within the limits of what Poulantzas terms the State's relative autonomy, the bureaucracy assumes a specific role. It can intervene within it, but this intervention is neither the cause nor the main factor in determining the autonomy of state practice. It is in the very structure of the State that this relative autonomy is inscribed and which makes possible the bureaucracy's specific role.

Poulantzas offers an analysis of the actual material framework of the structures and relations of the State which condition its intervention and serve to limit the practices of state personnel. It is this framework which must be taken into account in order to understand state managers' position in affecting change. Leaving aside the many unresolved debates about the work of Poulantzas, his contribution provides a robust alternative to traditional political science and public administration.

This theory also argues that consciousness and particular historic conditions are key to finding out what, if any, progressive role state managers can play. Poulantzas suggests that state bureaucrats do exercise a degree of relative autonomy but that this is both conjunctural (i.e., specific to time and place) and constructed by a particular articulation of economic, political and ideological structures and relations.

To further advance the question of progressive management moves research toward empirical study. Possibilities for progressive practice need to be firmly grounded in the world in which managers find themselves rather than in one where they might wish to be. It sounds rather obvious, but much management time and anxiety is spent constructing a practice for somewhere different than the agencies in which we find ourselves working: ones with different staff, more money, fewer and different clients, supportive public and communities. One way of avoiding this idealist tendency is to take seriously the material experience of managers and the changing state structures in which they find themselves.

With the aim of doing this, I undertook the research on which this article is drawn. The aspect of the study produced here addresses how people managing state social service organizations on two sides of the Atlantic—Québec (Montréal) and England (Devon)—in the mid-1980s, experience their relationship to the public and to elected power. The experience is of course different in the two places, and conditions in both are also different now than then, but they both contain lessons for constructing a more progressive future.

Welfare in the Eighties

We need to look briefly at the conditions social service managers faced in the eighties. Managers in both countries, where this research was done, were directly involved in a much wider process of change than merely the constant reorganizations they faced within their own social service organizations. This process of change was tied to reorganization of the State in both England and Québec, reorganization attributable to chronic and cyclical crisis in Western social and economic structures.

These managers did not personally initiate this change but they felt and were expected to take responsibility for it because of the direct impact on their institutions and jobs within them. Their simultaneous experience of power and powerlessness is an important characteristic of middle managers' structural position. How managers make sense of this position and take seriously its limits and opportunities is key to their participation in turning policy and legislation into real changes in practice.

The changing role and cost of welfare services continues to be central to political debate. Whereas in the seventies it was argued that the costs of services could no longer be sustained, in the nineties the costs of failing to provide services is beginning to mount. Thus the uncertainty and pessimism of the eighties welfare period faced managers with a very different set of circumstances from those which accompanied the creation of the unified social service agencies in England and Québec in the early seventies. In turn, the nineties may again offer some basis for optimism, but this can hardly be taken as inevitable.

Growing Politicization of Management

In Devon, there is a recognition of the influence that Thatcher's government is exerting on the conditions in which Social Service Departments (SSD) are managed. As one term of Thatcher drew to a close and the second began, the focus in local authority social services was on increasing financial controls. Spending money became itself a political act, placing the traditional values of Shire Tories in conflict—their loyalty to the party testing a traditional paternalism towards the old and needy. Organizational efficiencies are seen as a solution to these political problems and managers in the County Council SSD experienced the Thatcher revolution in the form of management consultants and reorganization. It is a tactic that the Conservative government has relied upon nationally, as well, preferring its speed and flexibility to the longer harder slog of breaking the hold of the civil service.[3]

The experience disrupted the confidence that people previously placed in social democratic and evolutionary processes of change. Change became harder to accept as solely the evolutionary product of processes of development, gradual, uncontested and uncontestable. Issues which these managers believe should lie in the purview of administration are becoming subject to a form of politics very different from the way Conservatives have run the County in the past. National party imperatives have penetrated in specific ways the operations of the local party and its management of the local authority. County party structures are called upon to develop national policy and ensure its dissemination across committees and in the Council chamber. The traditional relationship between Members and officers, policy and politics, has become itself a subject of the Government legislative programme and struggle for change.

In Montréal's English community the experience of growing politicization is more complex, with professional experiences becoming inextricably interweaved with broader changes in social and cultural life. Managers describe their professional experience of this wider political change in Québec as a 'New Reality'. In professional terms, it is described as containing three main elements: first, a feeling that power is increasingly concentrated in the Ministry of Social Affairs and its Regional Councils; second, that the social work profession and its methods are being replaced by technocratic methods of planning and resource allocation; and third, that the range of social intervention is increasingly controlled through demands framed in specific client group legislation, such as Youth Protection. These three elements together combine to colour managers' experience of this new reality as one where their power and 'autonomy', as well as that of their institutions, is being radically and politically undermined. The experience of the politicization of management takes on very personal meanings in the highly charged atmosphere of Québec's language relations. This daily experience of life in the province is impossible for managers to separate from their daily professional life. The 'new reality' is thus not merely technical nor political but experienced in a very personal and threatening way.

> I have to question the good faith of those people (the Regional Council). I have just read James Mitchener's

South Africa, and the parallels that I made in my head. And when they started to dispossess the coloureds and black people in South Africa and some of the strategies that are devised here to alienate the anglophones. To me its all part of the same thing...I think some of the Francophones, rightly or wrongly, are trying to get even with the English.

This is the background, and the foreground, for how managers are likely to experience a relationship to the public in both Devon, and in English Montréal. In both places public sector managers enjoy less than widespread popularity and support for the jobs that they do, the institutions that they run, and the clients they are intended to serve.

Managers' Experience of Democracy

Managers' experience of elected power is tied to working in a state hierarchy where change follows elections; it is introduced through legislation and executed through a set of superior/subordinate relationships. New policies are brought down from above in the form of orders, guidelines, instructions. In state institutions, authority is exercised through a chain of bureaucratic command. The size, range, and centralized nature of political decision making, to varying degrees in both countries, makes this a conventional means of organizing power.

Bureaucratization is a relatively recent experience for social work. Only since the reforms in the early seventies, in both England and Québec, have social workers been fully integrated into the State as 'local government officers' or 'civil servants'. These managers are a product of these reforms, themselves created as a by-product of large comprehensive social service departments. In both countries one of the criticisms of the reforms of the seventies was the growth of 'bureaucracy', with an increase in management structures and in the financial costs of administration. At the same time, all the new management structures and procedures seem to produce neither the effective organization of service nor desired changes in policy/practice.

Social workers are criticized for making bad managers, the social agencies for being badly managed, and calls for greater 'management competence' and more training are heard on both sides of the Atlantic. In my view, although the issue of 'management competence' is an important recognition of how these organizations often do not work, it is too narrow a conception within which to consider the effectiveness of the new social service departments and the changes they were meant to bring about. It is not purely technical questions of management expertise but wider issues of democratic state power and its exercise in bureaucratic structures that need to be understood.

I will describe these managers' experience of hierarchy through which they experience electoral power in the execution of the 'public interest'. I will consider their relationship to 'democracy' beyond this formal delegation from elected representatives and include the participation of users and potential users of services. Without the direct impact of market forces operating in the economic sphere, in the realm of the State it is political forces which direct and shape state institutions. It is thus important to examine how managers experience these forces, and the ways they relate to them in their efforts to manage public services.

Professional and Managerial Autonomy

Personal autonomy is a highly valued idea for many professional managers. In Québec, it is seen to be slipping away in the ways described as part of the 'new reality', whereas in Devon, it is something some of the lower level managers and workers hope to get more of as a result of the department's decentralization. These experiences and expectations are relative ones, ones that managers form in relation to some idea about how much autonomy they would like to have enjoyed in the past.

This simple contrast between the experience and expectation of autonomy in the two places conceals a great deal about the politics of power surrounding social service professionals. Doing what you're told by those above you in the hierarchy—whether civil servants or politicians—is essential to the functioning of bureaucracies. Yet it is not consistent with what most social service managers believe should be a professional mode of decision-making.

When this bureaucracy is located in a democratic State, the material base of that authority is that of democracy and elections embodied in a set of institutions and statutes, relatively autonomous from the economy and social classes (Poulantzas 1978). Much professional thinking does not see state bureaucracy as derived from material forces in the same way, but believes it has a separate and distinct power in its own right. In Weberian formulations, it is this power of officialdom that elected representatives have to work so hard to control and over which sophisticated mechanisms of control must be built. Bureaucratic authority in industry can be regulated by the discipline of the market and profitability. This is not possible in the State, and from within this theoretical perspective, the bureaucracy becomes an independent power.

Professionals are sometimes seen in a similar way as a separate and potentially powerful independent force, and a tendency exists to see professional authority as more legitimate and admirable than the fetishized authority of position that is assigned to the bureaucracy. The result is an irreconcilable and destructive conflict between professionals and bureaucracy—not a very helpful formulation if you are interested in managing public services. It would seem more fruitful, and consistent with what we know about the State, to consider how managers do reconcile their ideas and experience of professional autonomy with their ideas and experience of democracy.

In the next few pages I will examine managers' relationship to the public, in Devon and Montréal, first, as they relate to politics and elected members, second, in terms of the influence of extra-parliamentary forms of democracy, and third, consider the significance of this experience for a democratic management of public services.

POLITICS AND ELECTED MEMBERS

Devon's Local Experience of National Politics

In Devon there is a connection to the national policy scene. Through the Association of Directors of SSD (ADSSD), a senior manager can participate in national professional debates, and some felt they could influence the decisions that affect local authority social service departments. This relationship to the corridors of power significantly affects how they felt about the social service leadership in the country and the County. One senior manager described how he feels part of it and is involved in what policies are developed.

> I'm constantly reminded that I can and do make a contribution to the national debate and it can have pretty substantial consequences, either beneficial or detrimental.

This manager has gained access to national debate and the Secretary of State through professional networks rather than exclusively as a result of his position in Devon. In his accounts the ADSSD and the Association of County Councils are described as avenues to the corridors of power, and the private lunch continues to figure as an important British policy-making tradition.

Nor did this manager feel that the election of the Thatcher government has changed these relations, or his ability to work cooperatively with the Department of Health and Social Security (DHSS). He has a faith in the 'collective common sense' that gives him confidence in future policy. In his view, whatever Thatcher's Conservatives may represent in terms of expenditure policy, when it comes to the substance of social policy the way forward was clear and consensual. In an experience constructed over thirteen years of social policy in the U.K., political ideologies do not really have much effect on the running of government. 'At the end of the day', reasonable 'men' see the common sense facts.

> The current philosophies that are being promulgated, either of the extreme right or extreme left, are political ideologies. And political ideologies can rarely be sustained in the cold light of day, and particularly in the cold light of facts. So the process is more one of cascading from a principle to the practice, and the process of cascading is also one of screening. And at the end of the day the political ideologies are related into common sense fact, and that's where you get consensus.

Given the history of the previous thirteen years of social democracy in English local government, this was an understandable perspective. But this manager was expressing not only an experience of how social democratic institutions have operated, but his belief in a universal principle that this is how 'common sense' exists outside of and ultimately overrules ideology. In his view, Thatcher's Conservatism represents no significant shift in that consensus nor threat to common sense. What this belief in 'consensus' and the power of common sense facts points to is the continuity between his own ideology and the social democratic faith which still prevails in the corridors of central government, at least within the DHSS.

Local Political Relations

Despite this social democratic confidence in facts and consensus, Thatcher's political project was having some effect on life in Devon. The most obvious was through central government control of local government finance. Though Thatcherism was experienced as an alien force in the shire, traditional loyalty to the party has so far overruled the desire for local autonomy and strong disagreement over many of the financing controls.

> I don't think it's Toryism that is the basis of their support. It's loyalty to Mrs. Thatcher. I think they'll always be loyal to the government, but always will reveal the inconsistency that as local people they're passionately concerned about the quality of local services and raise problems on behalf of their constituents and are alarmed about any threat to their autonomy.

As there was no significant opposition to the Conservative party in the County Council, politics took place within factions of the party which reflect different social groups in the social world outside the Council. Party loyalty and discipline does not operate at this level and what opportunity does exist to construct movement and change exists as a result of these intra-party divisions.

Yet officers find this 'absurd'.

> It's a funny place, you see, because the local council has thirty-five, thirty-six seats—thirty-five conservatives and one independent. So because they don't have any opposition, it's absurd, you've got perhaps three factions, you see. So it's very interesting…you get people who mix in a certain social world, and so on. So politics don't work down here the way they do in Bristol or London.

Different levels of the party did not always work together either, but were torn between identification with party and identification with locality. In Québec, there is considerable evidence that formal local government boundaries do not necessarily correspond to people's cultural and historical affinities. In Devon, the lower tier District Councils guard their independence from the County Council. And the tension between the Districts and the County is reproduced on a wider scale between the County and Central Government.

Nevertheless, the Conservative project is changing the officer/member relationship in Devon. A separation and distrust is occurring between radical right political forces, in this case with Thatcherism, and the bureaucracy. When faced with a bureaucracy that says that the policy change to which they are committed is impossible, politicians were left to look outside the state apparatus. They turned to the expertise and class forces they feel they can count upon to introduce new ways of doing things. For political and ideological reasons the right felt that business consultants carried out their policy objectives more reliably than the bureaucracy.

> All the evidence we were producing for the members to take to Mr. Heseltine [Secretary of State] he would say 'that's your officers. They obviously got a biased view. I would believe their story much more if it was looked at critically by someone outside the County.' So fine, it was a good tough thing. Am I right?
>
> Is it an effective and efficient way of administering social services given the nature of the services that you're providing and in light of the character of the County? Is it cost-effective, or has he been shooting us a line since 1970?

The suggestion that local government officers are biased is a new experience for these managers who normally see politicians in that way. For Thatcherism, attacking the authority and cost of state professionals and administration was, and is, central. The question of whether or not local services can be run more efficiently is a deeply political question and quite different from apparently similar social democratic cost-saving exercises of the past. Whereas social democracy may also be concerned with getting the best value for money, its overall political project was expansion and increased investment in state service, within the limits that economic growth would permit.

When officers speak confidently of the cost-effectiveness of the social service department, and 'the line they have been shooting since 1970', it is a line constructed in a different political climate, informed by a different ideology. Their current confidence appears to stem from the belief that something 'out there' is objectively and universally 'cost-effective'. That anyone can see. Any other way of seeing is just wrong, can be rationally disproved, and hence beaten. History, and management consultants, are demonstrating the error of their certainty and the fallibility of this perspective.

Local Democracy and Public Service

In principle, managers in Devon upheld the idea of democratic authority and the right of elected members to properly run the authority. They have a direct experience of elected power through the local council and its elected members. All of the managers described substantial contact with County and District councillors: senior managers through County and Area committees; middle managers through Area Committees, the Health Authority, case panels, and community meetings; and Team Leaders over local issues on their patch, committees, case panels, and enquiries about individual cases.

These working relationships are very different from the relationships to elected representatives that Montréal managers have, or rather do not have. County, Area, and local managers have to have a working relationship with the politicians who are their bosses; their ideas about democratic accountability should stem from this real experience, as well as the abstract principles expounded here.

> Any Chief Officer needs to constantly remind himself, that no matter how powerful other people think he is, and no matter how powerful he may think he is himself, that we work in an accountable democracy and that the final decisions are taken by the Local Authority elected members. That is what democracy is about. And long may it remain that way.

> It's not simply a question of being figureheads. The Committee is very much involved—as it should be.

When the discussion is abstract and philosophical, managers believe that politicians should be really involved and contribute to the debate. It is a clear and straightforward set of principles—managers do what elected members decide. If one finds that unacceptable, then one resigns.

> If policies, political policies, are developed which are totally abhorrent to you, then you've only got two choices—you fight and make your views known, and if nothing happens, then you get out. That is really the reality of it. You've got to decide.

Whilst in principle this is how officers think democratic authority should operate, this is undermined by other principles. Officers were very critical of local democracy and believe it is not really very democratic nor representative of the powerless people that social services serve. One Senior manager tried to make the Area Service Committee (ASC) a more representative body than one which would have been possible drawn from the ruling party alone. In addition to the fourteen District and County Councillors on the ASC, seven co-opted members were appointed.

> Then we have seven co-opted members and they are not County Councillors at all. They are local people who are thought to have a special interest in social services and they come on and when they sit in Committee they are full members like the others. We've got two handicapped people actually as members, who feel they can represent the rights of the handicapped. So it's really quite a jumble.

The personal calibre of councillors was also wanting, in the view of many managers. Most councillors either aren't very interested, aren't very bright, don't have the time, or are irretrievably reactionary.

> They're a mixed bunch. You can pick out a few that you think are worth concentrating on. They've made some very

> sweeping statements and they've got an opinion about certain issues, and the others, they don't give a shit. You might as well concentrate on the ones that are looking for information and are interested.

At a local level team leaders questioned Councillors' ability to really understand and represent the community and its needs.

> You've got to look at some of the facts and figures about local council elections where you get something like fifteen or twenty percent of the population voting, so you've got to ask whether they're representative or not, in the first place.

Some managers working for local government believe that there is nothing democratic about it at all.

> It's just the whole system. It's all good on paper that you're ultimately responsible to 'the people' via the elected representative but unfortunately in practice that isn't what happens. It's like the judicial system, 'tried by your peers' and all that, well you're not. Although, as I say, it sounds all very good and democratic—it isn't really.

Ideas like this are common in contemporary British society but they take on a particular meaning for those working for local government. What is the whole thing all about if there is nothing democratic about it? In business, you know you're working for a firm that is given a coherence, ultimately, in its relationship to profit and the market. In local government, it seems many officers do not experience elected members and democracy as a similar organizing force. In practice, this undermines both any relationship to the public's power and also the effectiveness of elected authority and state organization.

Keeping Politics Out of it

These professionals express the classic social democratic contradiction—to keep politics out of government. Politics are irrational and cloud the thinking of objective and disinterested parties. They disrupt the normal evolutionary nature of change and the good orderly management of the department. The ideological chains which construct what is 'reasonable' in local government operate at this level. Professional, effective, good and service-oriented practice is contrasted with practice which is political, cost-saving, self-interested, with no concern with service or standards. From many officers' point of view, they are the ones with the vocational motivation, protecting the vulnerable members of society from the ambition, and the partisan and emotional attacks of politicians.

Politicians have the final say in a government bureaucracy which draws its immediate power and legitimacy from elections. Yet these managers experience and respond to democratic authority as if they had a separate base of power, when they do not. They have an empirical knowledge of the institution, and wider professional knowledge about running institutions and social services, and the facts of social need. By drawing upon this professional expertise, officers felt justified in being highly critical and dismissive of politicians and trying to keep the management of the department away from them.

To summarize Devon managers' relationship to electoral democracy: they do not seem comprehensively alienated from either national or local democratic politics. Chief officers felt they have a role in national debates and have influence with previous and current government ministers. All the managers had personal working relationships with County and District Councillors. In principle, managers acknowledge politics and the formal legitimacy of representative democracy. At the same time, they questioned the Conservative party's ability to represent the groups that social service serves, and criticized the ability and motives of many councillors. In practice, they used their professional position to block political initiatives that they strongly disagreed with. At the front line, they did what they could to keep members out of decisions about individuals and families.

Montréal Managers' Relationship to Politics and Politicians

In Québec, managers relate to state authority not through politicians, but through employees of the Regional Council. The Council is in turn directed by a Board appointed from interested constituencies (voluntary sector, socio-economic groups, municipalities, hospitals, residential centres, Local Community Service Centres, Social Service Centres, Lieutenant Governor representative, etc.). The political culture of language in Québec works against these otherwise highly participatory arrangements.

Representation for health and social service bodies is organized on a region-wide basis from particular corporate interests, ostensibly ignoring language and the smaller units of locality. At the Regional Council the collective influence of the English community is not very powerful as a bloc, for each English institution participates according to its function, as residential centre, social service centre, or hospital. In relating to the 'democracy' of the Regional Council, Ville Marie managers do so as managers of a Social Service Centre working with other Social Service Centre managers.

Outside Québec, it is normal for public services to be organized on the basis of the service they offer to the public rather than language or ethnicity, but in the eighties the English do not experience this arrangement as very democratic. In these structures their wish to defend what they see as the interests of the English community will inevitably be undermined by the numerical supremacy of the French majority. The challenge would be for them to organize across divisions of language and ethnicity on issues of public service, but the experience and position of English managers makes this difficult.

Although the division between politics and profession is obscured through a long hierarchy between the National Assembly and the institution, it is nevertheless experienced as highly political. The hierarchy from the Ministry, to the Region, to the institution, means that local managers have little contact with provincial politicians or the National Assembly. The separate social relations between English and French community outside the State mean that there is little informal contact either. It leaves Ville Marie managers feeling outside the political leadership and running of the province's social services. It is very different from the contact senior managers in Devon develop through professional and local government associations. As far as most Ville Marie managers are concerned, their position is affected by changes in government and their hope for the future rests with the Liberal party, in opposition at the time of these interviews but now in power. What limited information and contact they do have with the National Assembly is often through the Opposition.

Despite managers' experience of the Regional Council as a powerful body, its statutory powers are limited to coordination and advice. It has few executive powers and works either through creating consensus amongst its service institutions, or through recourse to the Ministry.

So the processes going on within the Regional Council are highly 'political' in that peculiar way of bodies with no real power, and are conducted by non-elected officials. This body is experienced by most managers at Ville Marie as an oppressive, if inevitable, part of life. It is quite separate from the professional concerns they have about running their centre effectively.

> All the other stuff, on the whole, I think is political, it really is political at the regional level.

Ville Marie's Ideology of Public Service

Some of the powerful ideas held by these managers about being public sector employees are deeply oppositional. Some describe how unpleasant it is to work for the State and how bureaucracy is a life-stifling and authoritarian form of organization. At the same time, in principle, electoral democracy has legitimacy and most state managers believe that accountability is a reasonable and necessary part of democratic government. Whatever else, it is the only way to justify the enormous cost of social services.

> However, there's a new reality in terms of money. I think accountability is something the government has a right to ask for because of the tremendous costs of developing social services.

> You could almost look at the government as a shareholder or Board of Directors in a private corporation, they want accountability, they want to know how the money is spent and we give them all the benefit of the doubt that they're really well-intentioned. There are times when we can doubt that they're really well-intentioned, but look....

Though they reluctantly give agreement to their political employers' right to accountability, some managers accept that the constraints being passed onto them by the Ministry and the Region are constraints that the Government itself has no choice about. They recognize that money is limited, and that in that context Ville Marie is relatively well-off.

> It's true that Ville Marie and the anglophone agencies were well-staffed and well-organized and had good services. I don't think it's possible for the government to say that we will have the exact same level of service across the province. I don't think the money is there. I don't think the capacity is there, they can't look at increased taxes...

Getting control of public expenditure and rationalizing the distribution of resources across the province is what many managers feel underlies the 'new reality' and reinforces its inevitability. These managers feel very far removed from and powerless to influence the political process by which decisions about public expenditure are reached.

> I think that ballgame is going on thirty-seven miles above my head. There's no way that I can be involved in it or influence it. I get informed of what's going on. Really that ballgame goes on with René Lévesque[4] and down, and how much money Québec has is really the bottom line.

Local managers face Regional Council decisions which rely not on formal authority alone but on political power backed by a material force such as the budget. Unlike in Devon, there is less faith in the freestanding power of facts and rational argument in determining decisions. Ultimately, the Ministry can withdraw the budget and effectively overrule any professional or philosophical objections. As one senior manager put it,

> What do you do when you're in a situation like that? You don't get the money. Schools are the same thing. When they decide to take them away, we're going to fight like bloody hell with every professional and philosophical reason why they should be maintained. And we have in fact successfully developed a very sophisticated argument at

> the ACSSQ. If they're going to listen to us fine, if they don't?...I don't know what it will get us. I really don't.

Most managers at Ville Marie have come to accept that there is no money and little way of influencing government spending priorities. With this acceptance and sense that there is nothing they can do, the new reality has to be accepted as unchanging and unchangeable. This is how they feel about the Québec outside their organization, and it comes into what they feel is possible in its internal management.

Doing What You're Told

Despite their position in charge of a large social agency, these managers do not feel they are running very much and certainly not a bit of the State. In fact some associate their experience of bureaucracy and powerlessness as an inevitable, if unfortunate, by-product of social democratic change.

> I would be more concerned if they got away from the kind of social philosophy that I think has always been here, especially with a social democratic government. They've been doing a lot of good programs. I think they're way over their heads in wasting, in spending money, but overall I think it's been a good approach to social problems. Where we've paid the big price is that we became civil servants. It's normal now that we're public service, and so hierarchical structures in the government make the decisions to say what direction we should go and that's what we do.

While social democracy is seen to be a good thing, as a philosophy to deal with social problems, it comes with having other people make the decisions and tell you what to do. It may be 'social' in the sense that more money is spent on services, but social democratic change is experienced as the opposite of 'democratic'.

> We have to recognize the fact that we are no longer a private agency. We are a parapublic agency that is less and

> less para and more and more public with a clearly mandated mission that's contained in law and by the Ministry. And while the Ministry does not deliver service they do call the broader shots. 'This is what a CSS does and this is what you must do.'

At the lower end of the management hierarchy, a social work supervisor considers it quite normal that if she chooses the security of wages, rather than self-employment, she becomes a civil servant and loses traditional professional autonomy.

> I feel I'm able to do enough of what I want within the constraints of a government organization. If I wanted to be my own boss, then what am I doing getting a government pay cheque? I should work in private practice. And I don't have the gumption for that, so I've got to take the constraints of being a bureaucrat.

It is a minority of managers who either accept the role of civil servant or who reluctantly accept the loss of autonomy in exchange for the social good of social democracy. The English social work community in Québec, with both its professional and ethnic experience of power, has not found the transition to faithful civil servant an easy or pleasant one. Most managers show continuing opposition to the government's direction.

Hostility to the 'new reality' is tied to the hostility to 'the kind of government' in power. For those who do not accept being a member of the civil service, the government is experienced as highly centralized with controlling ways of working. They experience a polarized relationship with the government and a conflict with their political bosses that is clear and unambivalent. It is a powerful expression of what many managers feel it means to work for the Québec State in the mid-eighties.

> That may be partly the times that we're living in and the kind of government we're having to live with...we're dealing with a highly controlling, centralized government that wants to be in control of everything and is the nub sitting there drawing up individual autonomy and even traditions

> that used to exist and pulling it into itself. It's like a spider sitting in the middle of its web. That's how I feel.

This is the typical experience expressed by Ville Marie managers about the government they work for, and the force directing the changes that they refer to as the 'new reality'.

What Autonomy?

Although Ville Marie managers sense an increase in control from above, a few felt that they retain some control over the means by which policies are implemented. As one senior manager put it 'he who pays the piper calls the tune', but there is room for improvisation.

> If I'm drawing a pay cheque, that will largely colour my thinking and what I do. But it can only control the substance of what you do, not the methodology. Therefore once they said 'you shall deal with childrens' substitute care', I think we have all kinds of freedom with regard to deciding how. We still have a certain *marge de manoeuvre.*

In terms of formal relations to authority, the work these managers do is meant to be defined and directed by those above them, but as in Devon, this formal authority is not effective in ensuring that the democratic will is carried out in practice. For although acutely aware of controls and with reluctant acceptance of a more modest professional role, they nevertheless do what they can to subvert political authority. Managers use the bureaucratic 'stall' to block policies being implemented. Stalling doesn't get positive action and therefore is not powerful in a positive sense, but by doing nothing, or causing delay by doing a 'comprehensive' 'professional' job, action can be prevented from happening. Sometimes through stalling, managers get their way. The Ministry gives up or is diverted by another pressing issue, or something else happens that changes the situation.

> The overall direction is given by the Ministry. The only thing we can do is negotiate the how. A lot of it is stalling and in some way stalling for a better deal.

These managers may not have the class experience or history of a British Cabinet Secretary, nor are they operating in longstanding social democratic institutions. Hence they may have a more limited set of possibilities for obstruction.

Nevertheless, since the Castonguay reform was introduced in 1971, they have managed to prevent most of its recommendations from being processed. These managers have prevented Ville Marie from being merged with the French and Jewish agencies into one social service centre for Montréal.

Very few Ville Marie resources or energies have been invested in developing Local Community Service Centres in their neighbourhoods, and Ville Marie still has no territorially-based mandate nor budget. In this negative sense, Ville Marie managers have managed to survive with their agency intact—if changed. They have some experience of getting their way; getting their way to be left alone to do things as they always have done, with the professional innovations which catch their interest.

In this period, Ville Marie managers were involved in organizing alliances with other social service centres in the province, through the Association of Social Service Centres of Québec. The English network of health and social service institutions also meets together to develop common strategy in regard to the Ministry and the Region. Altogether there is growing evidence that the English community is getting better at organizing as a minority pressure group within the province, but this should not be confused with running a part of the State.

To summarize Ville Marie managers' relationship to electoral democracy: they hold different and shifting ideological positions about the 'new reality', its legitimacy, and its potential for welfare services in the future. Some individual managers are ambivalent about working for the Parti Québecois Government; depending on the particular issue and circumstances they will be for or against. There are those who accept the materiality of the 'new reality' and are prepared to see the need for hierarchy and the merits of technocracy. They point out there is greater rationality in the distribution of resources, greater uniformity in the way clients are treated, more safeguarding of rights and entitlement to service. For others, it is the price to be paid for the security and salary of a civil servant.

On the other hand, there is the anger of a profession that feels that it is losing control of the present and future of social service provision in the English community. For most English professionals in the last Parti

Québecois government of the 1980s, a sharp line of conflict exists between Ville Marie and those above it in the hierarchy.

Each of these experiences, from out-and-out hostility to abstract intellectual conviction, contain serious limitations from the Government's point of view. Neither pole, nor the range of experiences in between, suggests that the government can expect much active help from this group of their cadre to make the new reality real.

Extra-Parliamentary Democracy

If most managers do not encourage elected politicians to be involved in directing public services, do they have other more direct relationships to the public? Other forms of social organization have emerged outside the State since the late sixties in England and Québec. Some of those interested in local state institutions see these movements as having an important role to play in making services more responsive to the needs of the community, and ultimately, in changing the social relations between the State and citizenry. From this perspective, the extent to which social movements outside the State can influence the form and content of social provision will determine the transformation of state organizations. The State can only be transformed by overcoming its separation from society and changing its relationship with the people. It cannot be done from the inside alone.

According to theorists such as Castels (1977), it is around local collectively organized services that the new social movements spring up and struggle. It is the contemporary social meaning and experience of the 'urban'. In Britain, Saunders (1981) applies Castel's theory and argues that local state services are more open to pressure from social groups than other parts of the State such as central state departments of the Treasury and Trade and Industry which are closer to the pressure of the market and the city. He sees local state institutions as potentially more democratic, and thus more likely to be subject to working class pressures, as constituted through fragmented consumer interests.

In Cockburn's study of the London Borough of Lambeth (1979), the 'local State's' unresponsiveness to social groups' demands, as well as the demands of elected Councillors, lead to her analysis that local government is not as responsive to the needs of local people as had been claimed by its advocates. In Cockburn's view, it is becoming the local State, subject to the same imperatives and constraints as the institutions of the central State.

In Québec, Vaillancourt (1983) uses similar criteria to assess the responsiveness of the newly established Regional Councils, and their corporate decision-making structure. He concludes that under the governments of both Bourassa and Lévesque, participatory arrangements in the Regional Council have not served to channel local pressure and demand up to the government, but rather have brought more government control down to the community. The research of Divay et al., (1979) makes similar conclusions about the influence of the community over decentralized state service institutions.

Social work has an important tradition of community work which intervenes to organize communities to meet their needs. This has taken different forms over the years, but in the seventies it identified local state services as an important target of protest and demands. In England, the Community Development Projects often came into conflict with local authorities over planning, housing, education, and social service issues. In Québec, the anti-poverty movement, and organizations of tenants and neighbourhoods saw social work agencies as sources of money, staffing and protection.

Both Seebohm and Castonguay devoted portions of their reports to these social movements and what they saw as the important relationship between them and social work practice. For both Commissions, the 'community' existed as more than a bundle of individual psychological and social problems. The new social service departments which followed from the recommendations of Seebohm and Castonguay were to be community-based in recognition of the important influence of the local community on social problems that would be brought to social services.

Managers' accounts of their relationship to elected democratic power show that they are critical of its legitimacy, its ability to represent social service clients, and that they doubt the motives, knowledge and commitment of elected local representatives. Now I will briefly explore managers' experience of social forces outside the State: do they relate openly to what might be considered more legitimate democratic forces such as individual and organized clients and community groups?

Wendy Thomson

Devon Managers' Relations With Clients

The more senior the manager in Devon, the less contact he has with clients. Decisions where there is a high degree of risk involved (i.e., risk that the department or social worker will be criticized publicly) are authorized by the director and in some cases, by sub-committees of elected councillors. Every management level has oversight of parental contact in child abuse cases, and contraceptive advice for children in care. Area Directors also clear decisions to place children in out-of-county facilities, largely due to costs involved. Divisional Directors are involved in getting meetings and decisions to go for care proceedings, as well as 'hairy' child abuse cases. Team leaders are closest to the front line, and through supervision have management's most direct client contact. Being too removed from client contact, from the front line where the *real* social work is done, is a worry for some. In professional mythology, giving up your last case is a rite of passage on the slippery slope to management sell-out. Managers want to keep their hand in as practitioners for as long as they can. One Devon Team Leader continues to carry cases, though his superiors have told him not to.

> I still have a couple of cases now that are a hangover from the team leader days. When I was a team leader I had seven or eight cases. I did that deliberately because I wanted to keep my mind in as a practitioner. But when we reorganized just over twelve months ago and I became a Principal Team Leader the A.D. made it quite clear that I would have to drop my caseload...It was a painful bit for me.

Clients are cases, and cases are the units of production to be managed in large state social services organizations. That is the prime relationship these managers have to clients. They have to know how many they've got, their status, be careful not to lose the tricky ones or invest too much time or money in one type rather than another. One of the team leaders has a chart of different coloured cards on his wall which represents the cardex file on each of his team's cases. It is his relationship to clients.

> This is as far as mechanization has gone and this is as far as I can cope with. All the cases that come in have different colours for different client groups...the green are elderly

the blue are children and families. The pink ones are child minder applications. That colour yellow is mentally ill, and that yellow is matrimonial supervision.

Most of the relations with clients goes on in these managers' heads in categories that have assumed professional meaning; the elements of people's experience that defines them for the institution—the six client group categories of children and families, under fives, elderly, mentally ill, mentally handicapped, physically handicapped. These are the cat- egories in which the community is discussed at management meetings and in policy debate. They are discussed as separate and distinct groups, inevitably in competition with each other for scarce department resources. Managers take up the cause of one or the other as the needs of one group come into and out of focus. 'Priority' groups for community care are still seen as under-provided for compared to children.

'Client groups' in turn grow into 'bodies of professional knowledge' or specialisms, which have to be protected if the needs of those groups are to be properly met. One Assistant Director describes the specialist 'knowledge' associated with children and families, elderly, physical and mental handicaps, and mental illness. For this manager, making sure these client groups get service means making sure that bodies of specialized professional knowledge aren't lost, and thus, that professional specialization is not lost.

Relating to Organized Clients in Devon

In Devon, there are voluntary groups that represent the interests of social service consumers. The Director meets regularly with the Council of Voluntary Organizations, MENCAP, and others, to get 'the client perspective'. There is a public relations aspect to this contact: in one manager's view, it is important to get to these groups with his account of events in the department before the trade union does. These groups are seen as an important forum outside the department that influences it inside. A number of Area, Divisional, and Team managers sit on the management committees of voluntary organizations, and some of their members are co-optees on the Social Service Committees.

Client surveys are another way the department gets the client perspective, and the research department had recently done one in North Devon which was quite critical of the department.

But neither clients, nor community groups, were either asked or expressed their views over the department's reorganization into 'patch'. The reorganization of the department is understood to be a professional preoccupation and initiative.

> There wasn't pressure from consumers. Patch was very much talked about. It was being written about in the journals. It was an idea gaining momentum, but in professional circles. There was no indication of consumer interest.

Two senior managers believe that clients and the community have a completely instrumental relationship to local services. They do not care about *how* services are organized, as long as they are organized and they get what they want when they want it.

> There is some attention given to noises that groups like MENCAP make, but that's mostly about services to be delivered, not how they're delivered or administered. 'All I care about is the dustman coming to collect my rubbish. I don't care about how it is organized.'

> The clients do not come to the department to get a service on local government finance or how you run your personnel or who types your letters. They come to get a service that's going to give them benefit—social worker or a home help or whatever.

Not only are clients' views described as 'noise', but because these managers assume that clients are not interested in how services are organized, they cannot be expected to know what their needs are even if they were to be asked. This belief provides a good reason not to ask. It follows on, of course, that if the public was to be asked, they might not want any social services at all.

> I'm quite sceptical of client participation. It's not that I'm saying that we know everything and what people need,

but I doubt that clients would know what they want if they were asked. I am afraid that many of them wouldn't want any service at all.

This is surely a worrying state of affairs for the future of the service. How long can managers expect to provide a public service that no member of the public knows how to want, and if they did know would refuse it? No wonder some managers feel it is best to keep as instrumental a relationship to clients as possible and no relationship to the public.

This aversion to involving the public is not only a matter of principle, but has direct impact on the service. The attitude is embodied in service relationships between the department and its clientele. The idea that clients are objects of production, rather than subjects, becomes, in reality, a denial of their agency and follows through in decisions that are taken for the sake of administrative efficiency, such as taking pension books from the elderly. One professional advisor in the department finds this trend worrying.

> One of the worst decisions we made was to take away pension books from people in residential care. It was a decision made on an administrative basis, so anyone who goes into residential care has their pension book handed into the area office and the area office then cashes their pension books and pays pocket money back to our residential clients.

Some younger managers experience the participation of organized groups as a valuable contribution to the running of the department. This Principal Team Leader gives them information so they in turn can attack the department. He rejects the idea that such organized groups, like elected councillors, aren't representative.

> There's a foster care association which is very vocal and I encourage them probably by giving them a lot of ammunition to fire at us, because I think we need firing at sometimes. But there is a criticism that they only speak for the minority. There are probably about a hundred or so foster parents in the Division and there are probably only a dozen

> people who are in the association, so very often what they say gets knocked down by social workers because they say they are only talking for a minority, and the vast majority, because they're very quiet, must be very happy. Now I don't think that's the case.

A few managers support participation of client groups but they do so against the dominant closeness of the institution.

Relations With Community in Devon

A few managers take a broader perspective about the world outside the SSD. They tend to be in the urban area of the County and have a clear idea about the importance of the 'inner city' community and their relationship to it. It is a view that is shared by this particular Divisional and Area management, and provides the vision for their commitment to change to a patch system of working. One team leader covers an area of three communities, each of which, has a community council which he hopes the SSD will join after his team is decentralized into patches. He approaches his team management rather differently from many of the others. He doesn't believe in counting cases, nor looking into the social service department for an indication of social need. He looks forward to decentralization to develop a new community based approach, 'still in its infancy'.

> I measure our work not in terms of cases, 'cause that's irrelevant really', but in terms of social need. How you measure that is in its infancy really. It has just started to be done as a result of this reorganization and because that's the way we're going to work now, thank God. You actually measure need according to not just what happens in social services, but you start to ask the people in the housing department about the problems they've got, start to ask the education department about the problems they've got, and local communities about things and then you can assess the workload that is likely and the needs of the clientele.

But other managers have a very confused experience of the community and their relationship to it. In the more rural Districts, professionals are ambivalent about communities, the more tightly knit they are, the greater the ambivalence. Paradoxically, some managers seem to feel that community social work won't work where there are communities.

> When I say Beesam is a tight community, I don't mean it's positive. I find it quite an incestuous situation. I can't imagine a good neighbour scheme working there because Mrs. Bloggs would be saying, 'I don't want that one up the road keeping an eye on me, thank you very much. I don't want her to know my business. She knows enough already thank you very much.'

> So when you come down to looking at that sort of thing, the actual community has got to be willing to have the rest of the community looking after them. There's too much nosiness already.

Of course we all know that you cannot do community social work in urban areas for exactly the opposite reasons—there is no community, not enough nosiness. It is rather a shame that the team leader dislikes this tight community, because according to the Divisional Director, it is the only 'identifiable community' in the Bay area.

> Beesam is the only identifiable community in the Bay which has suffered quite a bit because it is divorced by a few miles. All its services tend to be in the Bay, yet they have a very clear sense of identity, don't see themselves as part of the Bay, but have a sense of separateness, very conscious of their own worth as a community and nevertheless feel very hard done by.

The contradictions contained in the team's relationship to its community have clear material effects on the management of services and allocation of resources. For it seems you can't justify putting social work resources in 'real' communities—the 'need' just isn't there. We see here that the fetishism of the case count and the confusion between demand and need has a real material effect on what resources a community will get.

> We are looking at Beesam at the moment. That's what makes me so sad about identifiable communities, because geographically, it seemed to be a community, but when we looked at the referral rate it was quite low. Whereas we'd be saying yes, you could put a whole team out there, in the end we were saying maybe not. There isn't that amount of work.
>
> We don't serve them particularly well…Of course, because they don't have a team at the moment…

The identifiable community of Beesam is doing what it can to be identified as a place that might get a social service, but the team manager understands this as 'political' and therefore separate from social need for services. Community need seems to only count as long as it lies passively waiting to be discovered or surveyed. When need is expressed as a 'political' demand, it is considered illegitimate.

> We're hoping to do some surveys with the other agencies, like the schools or the G.P.s and there's a voluntary group out there called 'Beesam Do Care'. But that's very political.

On the other hand, there are the smashed communities where there is a whole set of different reasons why too much social work is not possible, or desirable. When she first arrived in Devon, this team manager described the deprived area she is responsible for as 'dependent'.

> Six years ago when I took over the team there was a really dependent feeling coming from the Area. Clients would ring up and say 'if you don't send a social worker I'm going to commit suicide'. Things like that. I used to say, 'Well if that's what you want to do, go ahead and do it'. And hopefully it would be all right afterwards.

Now clients don't call like they used to and the community is considered 'apathetic'.

When a youth and community centre was opened, despite their effort they 'can't get the community bit going'. Then the team undertook what they called the 'Effort Project'. They 'didn't actually do the project but we wrote about it'. Their thinking about doing it is, nevertheless, interesting.

> What we tried to look at was how we could put a different sort of input into the area. How we could make a more informal, casual contact with people. And it's such a deprived area that if you put one or two people out there, they could be drained. There isn't the job satisfaction, I don't think. So what we thought was that we would divide their jobs in half and they would work half in the very deprived area and half would be in something completely different that would give them a change and a bit of a balance.

If you can't put social workers in real communities, neither can you expect social workers to work in deprived communities. A rather odd relationship exists between social work managers and the members of the public who live in these communities.

Upholding Community Values

> There is a need to feel that as social workers they are representing the normative values of the community, but in recent years there is a lot of confusion about this mandate. Sometimes social workers feel that they are valued resources, other times that the community is not sophisticated enough to understand what they do, and others feel that if the community did actually understand they wouldn't be willing to pay for it. It is not the kind of warm confident feeling that would give you courage faced with an abusing member of the public or a disgruntled ratepayer.
> The one external message that professional managers have received is that they have an image problem. The experience of unpopularity may represent the seed through which to change managers' experience of the community and their relationship to it.

> We've got a very poor image—that we're not worth the money we're paid for. We've had a lot of strikes that go on indefinitely with no apparent effect.

What managers don't experience about community and clients is as important as what they do.

A third of the managers I interviewed in Devon managed not to mention clients, community, or cases even once. This tells us how removed from the outside world a manager can become in working for a SSD. It may also say something about managers' understanding of what social service management is. For this one-third, my questions about management had nothing to do with clients or the community: that is politics, or community work, not management.

On the other hand, managers spoke at length about the internal reorganization of the department, the detailed interaction between various levels of the hierarchy and subtleties of consultative processes with staff and trade unions within the department. This is a telling illustration of where the centre of reality is experienced by social service managers. Both ends of the accountability pole—politicians and public—are far away, and rarely seem to penetrate this world.

I have argued that establishing a relationship with the public which demonstrates the social value and efficiency of services is essential to the future of these services. This is a key management task if a progressive practice is to be developed, one which allows client and community more power—an active relationship to public services.

These managers see their jobs as very separate from their public who are merely another object to be planned for, another factor to be taken into the resource allocation equation. One is left with the feeling that the services are not 'public' in any real sense.

Ville Marie and English Québec

On the North American side of the Atlantic, Ville Marie emerged from a very different set of social forces which came together to produce the social democratic reforms of the late sixties and early seventies. How does this social service agency, which has quite recently moved from the private to the public sector, relate to its community, its clients and its locality?

Ville Marie has a powerful historical relationship to the English community. This is not simply background or context, as it is most often portrayed in organizational studies, but is a powerful personal reality for these managers and the people who work for them. In the past, the welfare leadership of the English community ran their own services. As the English community in Québec becomes a minority group in a political as well as statistical sense, this leadership is forced to recognize its changed position. One senior manager sees this quite clearly.

> They're still there with their mentality of fifteen years ago when they were dictating and controlling. They're dictating and controlling very little right now that's the reality.

The formerly powerful English community clings to the 'autonomy' experienced in the past. Its social work agencies have lost this power through integration into the State. This may inevitably be experienced as a coercive trend by many professionals, but in Québec it is strengthened by the experience that the State is run by a separate linguistic group. Unlike in Devon, all the Ville Marie managers describe a deep connection to the founding agencies. The memory of the agencies from which Ville Marie sprang is very significant—Catholic Welfare Bureau, Catholic Family and Children's Services, Family Service Association, Lakeshore Community Services, South Shore Community Services, Children's Service Centre. Although Castonguay was commissioned in 1966, the Act passed in 1971 and Ville Marie founded in 1973, the reorganization of the old agencies into Area Service Centres didn't actually happen until 1977 (West Island), 1978 (Centre City), and 1978 (South West). The memories of the period are mixed, though most workers remember the good old days.

> I dream of the old days. I would prefer the old days. I think that obviously in terms of money, social workers make more money now than they did ten years ago. But in terms of services I would have preferred that there was a government agency and also a private agency, or a partially funded agency to do counselling, to do some of the things that we cannot do right now and that is desperately needed.

Management arrangements seem to have been rather uneven in the old private agencies. There was substantial autonomy over the work that social workers would do. One Programme Coordinator compares it to the present system.

> It was horrible in that time. People were pretty autonomous about what they wanted to do. It was a pretty laissez faire kind of thing, so if somebody thought they had too much to do, that was all there was to it...They sort of met at team meetings and decided if they wanted this case or did not want this case.

How management control operated seems to have had mostly to do with the personality of the director and the style of the period. Looking back, these managers describe how they were managed in the private agencies in different ways—'the tyranny of the old agency run by a director who maintained control through unpredictability and constant crisis', or 'a laissez-faire approach that sometimes left you on a limb with the limb cut off', or the over-politicization of the early seventies.

Whatever the experience, moving out of these private agencies into the public mainstream has been traumatic. The early experience of what happened to the English community on the South Shore is pointed to as a concrete reminder of betrayal.

The Board of South Shore Community Services agreed to vote itself out of existence and integrate into Richelieu Social Service Centre. The guarantee to English language service never materialized to the satisfaction of South Shore English residents and this history is a living reminder of betrayal by the majority. Never again.

> The problem is that in the context of the Québec reality services to the English must be protected. I can't compromise on that duty.

To most Ville Marie senior managers the relationship between their service and the community is more than the instrumental one which Devon managers advocate.

> That's respecting the vision of the founding communities that brought Ville Marie into existence. I'm not saying that we shouldn't speak French, but that we should always be recognized as the English CSS. The administration and the Board must run in English. There's more to a service than the specific task of say a homemaker to a little old lady.

> The anglophone community should be permitted to say that this is their institution, the CSS should be responsive to their concerns and be in control of its destiny to the extent that it can. Whether this is misguided or not, I don't know. I may lose. But should this institution give up its heritage just because of the Bill 101[5] and because of the territory imposed by the MAS because it's more efficient? I don't think so.

These managers feel that the future looks far from certain for the survival of anglophone institutions and professionals. The service plans that the Ministry is trying to process are founded on further integration of services organized on a territorial basis. Experience is that even territories with a majority English population produce ostensibly bilingual institutions that are experienced as French.

> One of the big fears of staff is 'will the CLSC become francophone institutions?' even here. The francophone population of the West Island is building up. The anglophones are moving out and the francophones are moving in...And the CLSC Petersborough, although they have bilingual programs and services, basically, it's a French organization.

> I think the danger for us is that there won't be an anglophone institution fighting for the anglophone client population any more. It's not a problem for MM, they don't need anybody to fight, or stick up for their rights. The best example is the CLSC in Petersborough, which is what we consider to be an anglophone area.

In the view of some managers this relationship to the past and to community is a mixed experience, for whilst it is important it has produced enormous 'conflict' but no change and innovation.

> Really that's one of my biggest disappointments. There was a real opportunity to do different things. There was no tradition. We could have done things but rather than rock the boat and get some of those things done the attitude was always the

opposite—back off and maintain the status quo. There's been huge battles in the organization—its been characterized more by that than by any sort of cohesiveness.

A Strategic Relationship to the 'Environment'

Ville Marie has adopted a conscious strategy to move out of its historic isolation and relate to the rest of Québec, English and French. The 'environment' is considered an important element for analysis and intervention. Managers see some of the problems the agency is facing to be a result of not paying sufficient attention to the world around it, the world of the new Québec. Part of the senior management job is ensuring good communications and public relations.

> There's a considerable amount of time spent with the external media, with the press, and the communications part. Because we are the English CSS and there's been a lot of concern about the Government's orientation and the socio-economic indicators. Not only to ensure that the English agencies are seen as a network in terms of having a newsletter and that kind of thing, meeting with the directors and presidents of the anglophone agencies, and we're involved in a process with Alliance Québec. Then meeting with the Mayors, the MNAs and the Liberals and their organization.

The French community is a key part of this environment that they feel that must learn about, make contact and work more closely with.

> I think we have brought Ville Marie more in touch with the CRSSS process and the ACSSQ. I've been to every ACSSQ meeting. I used to just listen but now I intervene with my point of view. We didn't use to get involved or see that as important. Now I do.

Not all the managers have changed their thinking in this way. Some of those buried in the middle of the organization, unable to speak French are not able to go out and participate in the service network.

> I get reports in French and I just tend to disregard them and not read them, because I don't have time.

A telling statement of middle managers' attitude to their Québec Government employers—weighty policy documents, social service plans, Ministry directives—these are not taken seriously but are 'disregarded'. Yet these professional managers are supposed to be responsible to the Government for executing its policies. Clearly many do not see this as their job, so who do they feel accountable to?

VILLE MARIE'S 'CLIENT ORIENTATION'

Dealing With Complaints

Ville Marie has a centralized mechanism whereby clients can make a complaint. All the managers were aware of its existence and how it worked, one of the systematic procedures that is well-established and adhered to. All complaints can go to the Director of Professional Services who conducts an investigation down the hierarchy where the worker, supervisor, and programme coordinator usually sort it out. This gives managers a different relationship to clients than those in Devon. In Ville Marie, it is the action of the client that results in the senior manager coming into contact with their problem, whereas in Devon, it is internal procedures that determine what goes up the hierarchy for management attention.

The experience of the volume of complaint varies, as does the seriousness with which managers respond to client criticism. A senior manager...

> Complaints, not necessarily formal complaints. That's very small. But enquiries, asking for a change of worker, or 'I wanted to be a foster parent and was turned down', that kind of thing.

Three Programme Coordinators have different views about the volume and meaning of client criticism.

> Surprisingly we aren't getting very many now...Really I don't take complaints very seriously because it's always a

> personality thing, rather than a poor job. Complaints come in batches. I would say about one a month but that involves meeting with the worker, talking to the complainer who usually by the time they come to me is on the ceiling, so that's a lot of work. Then talking to the worker who's got a complaint, so is on the ceiling. Meeting with them together to resolve the problem. I find that very stressful.

An important dynamic in clients' right to complain is that as the system of service delivery becomes more 'just', and the rationing system more technocratic, ordinary people can have a genuine need that is not being met, as a result of rules and regulations, the CSS's obliged to ignore them. So the problem of accountability to clients' criticism may worsen rather than improve. Given my argument that opening institutions to public criticism and influence is critical to progressive practice in the nineties, the risk of building complex professional defenses against client criticism and demand is a serious danger.

Client Philosophy

The most contact Senior managers have with clients is the idea of clients that they carry around in their heads, and for many the service philosophy is a strong one. It is at odds with the changing and more complex service delivery system that is being developed, which tends to classify clients into types and process them accordingly.

> My thesis is that our mission is social services to clients, whether they be first line, second line, or whatever.

As in Devon, there is a debate about what that service should actually consist of, and a feeling that social work has taken on an impossible job. In Ville Marie, this means working for months and sometimes years with casualties that are considered beyond repair.

> What happens is that we spend most of our energy working with people that the army triage system would simply leave to die. They're too seriously wounded…That's not to

> say that they couldn't be saved if you had the resources to
> help them, but based on the reality of what you have, you
> can't really do a whole lot for them.

There are two opposing poles that represent the profession's relationship to the agency of individual clients: the cases that are beyond repair, and the cases that get better by themselves. Social work seems to have no role with those who are either too badly wounded, or are not wounded enough. In this social service organization, people as cases are the unit of production and team managers describe people in the form of cases being bartered, if not exchanged for cash. Although people as cases are exchanged, unlike real commodities in the market, simulated commodities in the public service have a negative exchange value. Rather than competing to acquire cases to serve, Programme managers try to push cases onto other service units. Public service management involves managers in avoiding the public and in seeking to shift responsibility for service elsewhere.

> There's still a lot of discretion around but it's usually 'You
> don't want it, we don't want it. So who's going to get stuck
> with it?'

When social problems hit the news media, it is to Ville Marie that people officially turn. For example, in a situation of an abandoned newborn baby there is a contradictory message. On the one hand, the mother of the baby did not contact Ville Marie but preferred to leave its fate to fortune. On the other, members of the public approach the Director with enquiries and much advice about the baby's future.Ironically, in a case like this the first task is to determine whether the case would be allocated on a territorial or socio-linguistic basis, whether the baby was a French baby or an English baby, the responsibility of Ville Marie or Montréal Métropolitain (the French agency).

Client Participation

By law, the Social Service Centre is obliged to have a certain number of representatives of users and voluntary organizations on its

Board of Directors. Ville Marie established participatory structures at the same time as the Area Service Centres and included client advisory bodies at each point of service (Citizen Advisory Councils) as well as at the centre (Central Consumer Council).

The professional view of the success of this participatory structure is rather mixed. Some managers feel they are unrepresentative and not rooted in any real social movement or community interest. Some of the groupings are seen to be prone to sectarian conflict, personal nastiness, and general flakiness. According to one Area Service Centre Director,

> I think they should cut the whole Central Consumer Council. The whole CCC thing is just abysmal... Certainly it hasn't worked. I think probably it's a bad concept because what has already happened is, despite the philosophy of getting some kind of representativity, you get a small group of people—five if you're lucky—who just subsume the whole operation and are really representative of no one. Who do they represent? Who do they think they represent? And then they start feuding with each other. The more you're involved, the more bizarre you realize it is. It's a real horror scene. The CACs and the CCC are always at each others' necks. Unbelievable. Unbelievable.

This isn't the universal experience. Some CACs in other Areas are experienced as very positive.

> The CAC run projects and take up causes which the community considers are important. This is an excellent organization.

> This is a very strong verbal community. They have the political know-how to use their M.P.s. Suddenly they're sending all kinds of letters off all over the place. They can have an effect. They can have an effect more than I can because they're speaking supposedly for the citizens within the community.

> They're quite prepared to do that in this community. They've done it. It's been a tradition. And they're good at it.

At different times in the agency's history, there have been campaigns to mobilize the 'community' and 'consumers' in support of the agency—campaigns for children in care, campaigns to defend the rights of natural parents, campaigns against budget cuts, and to defend the anglophone institutions against integration into the *réseau*. The management approach of the Centre has been influenced by the organization of these campaigns which have quite different attributes and imperatives from a public service management approach. Some managers were sceptical of the value of this mobilization and would rather have seen their efforts put into more traditional managerial activity.

Management order and campaign mobilization contain a contradiction between being open, with all the chaos this potentially brings into the institution; and closing up, with all the weakness that this means for an organization under threat from forces inside the State to which it would be victim.

A different view is held by one manager who says 'I don't live with history and I'm not bound by history'. He holds the view that the relationship between clients and institutions is an instrumental one, similar to that of some senior managers in Devon. From this perspective, clients are seen to care only about getting the service; the form and control of its' organization is irrelevant.

> The senior citizen in Anjou who wants to be placed in an anglophone reception centre wants to be placed there. How he gets there, obviously the worker who interacts with him has to be able to respect his or her culture. I'm all for that.
>
> But whether the supervisor of that worker has to be an anglophone with a manager and a Board of Directors who are anglophone, is immaterial. I don't think the client gives a damn.

If the client doesn't 'give a damn' and managers feel it is not their job to persuade them otherwise, then the agency's relationship to its users is a passive one. This is not the relationship which Castonguay envisaged. It begs the question of how services become defined and needs recognized—a professional not a public concern?

Ville Marie Managers' Relationship to Locality

Whereas the francophone CSSs centralized in the mid-seventies and began decentralizing in the mid-eighties, Ville Marie went through a lengthy 'Area Service Centre Task Force' after its foundation, and with considerable community interest and involvement set up a structure of area-based offices. There is humour, as well as regret, about the limited relationship it is possible for social work teams to establish with the Areas they now cover.

> Well, our territory. We have a joke on our team that if it's anywhere from Atwater to World's End then it's ours. Another joke is the glazed look on the Metropolitan Expressway. When I was a line worker I thought I was living on the Metropolitan. It's crazy. You just see isolated people…It's very hard when you've got people knocking down the door. So there's not a whole lot of community work.

> It's quieter here. Away from the politics of Verchère. Other than that we're closer to our clients I guess. We're in the area. We can certainly empathize with our clients in terms of poor housing conditions (pointing to the chipped paint in his office).

Workers with special responsibility for certain ethnic groups seem to feel it is more possible to work on a community basis.

> Actually the Italian worker, the two actually are very good at making contacts in their respective communities for supports and resources. The Italian worker is now trying to set up a group with kids in the area in a church or school where the kids will be in their own community.

Cynicism may stem from expectations developed in the pre-Ville Marie past when social work teams had community organizers and a closer relationship to local tenant and neighbourhood groups. Nevertheless, managers serve on the management committees of voluntary organizations, other service establishments, and work jointly with churches and police on their territory. As in Britain, social workers in English Québec are beginning to worry about the strength of their support in the increasingly individualistic and ungenerous community of the 1980s.

> The community is asking for something very specific for the money it is paying. It's social protection in quite a narrow sense. In other industries satisfied customers are your best references. In our work, a satisfied customer is one who feels their problem is behind them and is never going to reflect or think very much of who helped, the kind of help they got, nor the need of other people for the same help.

Being a minority may bring the English community together to defend its institutions in a way that individual customers may not. Ville Marie's opposition to the rest of the Québec state network closes them off from the mainstream, but opens them up to the margins. As an oppositionary strategy this has its weaknesses, but it strengthens the position of clients and community in the operation of the Centre. There's nothing like a principled struggle.

> The whole issue of the right of anglophones to receive services in their language is a real issue to fight and to stand for what we believe, and I believe is correct.

But the struggle brings these managers into a relationship of isolation and conflict with the majority community as it is represented through the Québec Government; not a relationship of incorporation and accountability. In the late sixties the English community believed that it could no longer fund and sustain separate and autonomous social service agencies. It needed state help and broader public support. Ville Marie managers do not seem to be moving in that direction.

Conclusions: If Not Public Then *Whose* Management Is It?

The ideology and experience of both sets of managers demonstrate that they seek to isolate themselves from the material forces that construct their organizations. Both are public organizations which were meant to be run through a relationship to parliament and local government. They were brought into existence by legislation introduced by Governments in the U.K. and Québec elected with new social democratic programmes. It was a change in Government which constructed the two organizations and brought the positions these managers occupy into existence. Yet given their belief that politics is an inconvenience, middle managers find this democratic change an intrusion into their professional lives. They believe that management would be far more effective without political interference. In fact, the reverse is actually the case. For as long as managers continue to isolate themselves from political processes, they are doomed to be ineffectual in making progressive change.

In any period of increased rate of change representative democracy will enforce radical change on state organizations as effectively as it can. At times such as these, managers' general refusal to recognize that they are run by political forces becomes more difficult. The search for scientific and technical solutions becomes more frantic and more futile. This is manifested in different ways in the two social structures and their two social agencies. In Montréal, the idea that middle managers are in charge of their institutions is being challenged by the continuing reality outside as well as inside the State. In Devon, in the face of the radical Conservative change, managers attempt to organize their institutions around an idealist call for consensual progress.

The real historical situation facing these individual 'choices' is limited, and as I have pointed out, these are not revolutionary times. Public services are in a defensive position and it is understandable that those working within them adopt a defensiveness. But as long as service managers maintain separation and independence from the public and outside movements they will not involve themselves with the struggles of clients and community groups, except as they can use them to extend their own power.

It may feel safer on a day-to-day basis for managers to develop ideas and methods to distance themselves from the public, but hiding can hardly be considered a viable long term strategy for a public service. Nor is doing nothing. For one of the most striking aspects of talking to managers about their experience is their sense of lostness, their feeling that there is very little they can do, that they work in structures that cannot be counted upon and have jobs that cannot in any real sense be done.

It is a problem in which prevalent ideas about management play an important part. For as everyone knows, managers are meant to manage. It is their job not only to know about structure and order, but in fact to construct it out of chaos and disorder: to manage new circumstances and change through anticipating it and making plans that take it into account. Count the number of articles, conferences, courses which market themselves to contemporary managers under the slogan the 'management of change'. Change is the job to be done, the job that managers are meant to manage. To be progressive, it is a job that must be done in partnership with users and the public.

Others around them in the structure collude in the understanding of the position and power of management. Trade unions committed to limiting management power do so in the conviction that managers have in fact got some power to be limited.

The contrast between the material experience of most managers' professional lives and the ideology they hold about their roles is in itself a powerful source of dissonance. It is a dissonance that serves to further disable their ability to manage in the current conditions of welfare institutions.

This is a problem not only for those of us trying to do the job, but for those who expect us to be doing a job: those above us who are trying to deliver policy to the administration of the day; those below who look to us for leadership and support; and the clients and public who expect someone to be running the institutions they pay for, vote for, and on occasion, rely on. If the public service cannot be seen to work, the market will continue to appear as the only viable alternative.

NOTES

1. The research on which this article is drawn was undertaken with the support of Doctoral Fellowships from Health and Welfare Canada, and Fonds F.C.A.C. Québec. I am grateful for their assistance.
2. The population which Ville Marie was responsible for serving was subject to debate with the government. The Ministry wished to make Ville Marie responsible for a 'territory', whereas the Centre had historically a socio-linguistic mandate for English speakers.
3. Norton - Taylor writing about the changes brought about in the British Civil service as a consequence of the Thatcher era

Wendy Thomson

> ('Maybe, Prime Minister', *The Guardian*, 13/09/89)
> observes that the effect has been subtle and insidious. There
> has been no radical clear out of top personalities nor
> wholesale reorganizations of the Government machine. Prime
> Minister Thatcher has instead sought more alternative sources
> of advice, looking to businessman, to young political advisors,
> and academics, such as Sir Alan Walters, her monetarist
> economics advisor. In turn the way she has plucked out and used
> young civil servants has prompted widespread concern for the
> 'integrity' of the service.
>
> Of course such apparent concern for the 'integrity' of local
> government officialdom justified the British Government's
> Commission of Enquiry under Lord Widdicombe. This eventually
> lead to legislation (Local Government and Housing Act
> 1989) which seeks to control many aspects of local
> government conditions of employment and decision-making,
> including restricting the political rights of those working in
> local Government.

4. Premier of Québec at the time.
5. Bill 101: Québec's charter of the French language which was introduced by the Parti Québecios to protect the French language. It made French the offical language of the Province and restricted the use of English in public forum.

LIST OF ABBREVIATIONS

Devon
ACC- Association of County Councils
AMT - Area Management Team
DHSS- Department of Heath and Social Security
DMT- Divisional Management Team
DoE- Department of the Environment
IT- Intermediate Treatment
LASSA- Local Authority Social Services Act
OPCS- Office of Population, Census, and Statistics
RAWP- Resource Allocation Working Party
SMT- Senior Management Team
SSC- Social Services Committee
SSD- Social Service Department

Ville Marie
ASC- Area Service Centre (Ville Marie)
CESBEC- Commission d'Enquête sur la santé et le Bien-être sociale
Ch. 48- An Act Respecting Health and Social Services in Québec(1971)
CLSC - Centre Locale de Services Communautaire
CRSSS- Conseil Régional de Santé et de Service Sociale
CSS- Centre Service Sociaux
CSSMM- Centre Service Sociaux de Montréal Métropolitain
CSSSMM- Conseil de Santé et de Service Sociaux MontréalMétropolitain
DAS- Department of Administrative Services
DD- Divisional Director
DPM- Department of Programme Management
DPS- Department of Professional Services
DYP- Director/Department of Youth Protection
DPJ- Directeur/département de la protection de la Jeunesse
JFSC- Jewish Family Service Centre
LCSC- Local Community Service Centre
MAS- Ministère des Affaires Sociales
MSA- Ministry of Social Affairs
OB- Operations Board (Divisional Management Team, VilleMarie)
PC- Programme Coordinator
RRDD- Regional Resource Development Division (Ville Marie)
SSC- Social Service Centre
VMSSC- Ville Marie Social Service Centre *Ville Marie S.S.C.*

Chapter Three

LIMITS OF BUREAUCRATIC CONTROL: SOCIAL WORKERS IN CHILD WELFARE[1]

Linda Davies

In most welfare state countries the political, ideological and economic context for the practice of social work has changed over the last two decades or so, prompting debate amongst welfare theorists about what is happening and where we are headed. This essay will look at competing theoretical explanations of the contemporary organization and practice of state social work. In particular, I will take issue with the determinism of some theorists on the left. I will consider the proletarianization thesis which focuses on the labour process, that is, the way in which work is actually carried out in the welfare State. And I will consider a second explanation concerned with the ideological reproduction of capitalist social relations. In relation to welfare, this thesis focuses on the social control function of state social work.

Working from in-depth interviews with British practitioners in the area of statutory child abuse, I will argue that although both explanations account for some recent tendencies in state welfare structures, they are ultimately unsuccessful in coming to grips with social workers' day-to-day experience of practice. Further, the determinism of these kinds of analyses has negative political consequences for state workers and their clients. Indeed, they are characterized by a "crippling fatalism" (Leonard 1979). In the labour process explanation, social workers are subjugated through increased managerial control and have no opportunity to resist. In the social control critique, social workers are simply part of an oppressive and monolithic social order; they are the soft cops of the welfare state who police working-class families. While these analyses generate despair about any possibility of struggling "within and against the state," it is in the state sector that most social workers are employed and it is state social workers who deal with the majority of clients, especially non-voluntary clients.

The arena of welfare has often been discounted on the left; in the classic Marxist view welfare workers were politically insignificant by virtue of their location outside the real centre of struggle at the point of production. For those more concerned with ideological control, the welfare State and welfare workers were part of the problem; they were effective and willing agents of the dominant capitalist class. Thus, these theoretical accounts had nothing to offer state workers interested in contributing to progressive social change, except perhaps the injunction to quit. Workers developed icy attitudes toward theorists and academics, observing tartly that "it's all right for [them] to talk" (Cohen 1975).

When the welfare State came under attack from the right in the late seventies and early eighties in Britain and North America, the left found itself in the contradictory position of defending the very structures and services which it previously had condemned. Clearly, a re-thinking on the left was necessary. The left critique of the welfare State in Britain had, of course, been developed in pre-Thatcher England. The left at that time set itself in opposition to the received social democratic wisdom that social problems could be solved within capitalism given the right political will. Since the Second World War dominant social democratic ideology accepted the welfare State as basically sound but perhaps in need of fine tuning. In the face of apparent failures of the welfare State, for example in relation to child abuse, social democrats typically argued for more and better training, better management and more rationalized structures to promote effective decision-making. This ideology became the target of the radical right of Thatcher's Britain. In contrast to the social democratic faith in the welfare State, proponents of the new right argued for the freeing up of market forces and a dismantling of the 'nanny' welfare State. Since the ascendancy of Thatcherism, the left has been in disarray, unable to provide significant political direction. There is thus an urgent need to develop alternative analyses of the welfare State which draw on a dialectical analysis and emphasize contradictions in welfare structures and practices, thus avoiding deterministic paralysis. To this end I will examine some of these issues in relation to contemporary child abuse practice in Britain. I will begin by briefly highlighting some of the major shifts in the organization of social work in Britain in the last twenty years or so. Some of these have obvious parallels in North America.

The Changing Organizational Context for Practice

Since the late sixties social service organizations in England and North America have undergone a process of bureaucratization and centralization of managerial power and control. In England the Seebohm reorganization in 1968 resulted in the unification of social service structures and the adoption of a model of generic, family based intervention. As well, the basic units of local governments were made much bigger so large scale bureaucracies became the norm. In the seventies 'corporate management' was introduced into British local authorities. This allowed even greater centralization of power in fewer hands (Cockburn 1977; Benington 1976). Social service organizations adopted business management techniques (PPBS, MBO, cost-benefit analysis) from the private sector, which encouraged a greater distance between those who conceive and plan welfare services and those who carry out day to day practice (Tudiver 1982; Bolger *et al.*, 1981; Lesemann 1984; Davies 1985).

This restructuring of the State was accompanied by cutbacks in public expenditures for social welfare. In contrast to the massive growth and expansion of the welfare State in Britain which followed the Second World War, by the late sixties an economic crisis was apparent (Gamble 1982; Hobsbawm 1965; Gough 1979). Public spending was pilloried as the source of Britain's economic woes (Joyce *et al.*, 1985), and a period of retrenchment began in the mid-seventies which continues today. Thus, the resources available to front-line state social workers are severely constrained while at the same time the economic crisis has yielded massive unemployment, increasing social problems and a greatly expanded potential client population. In the increasingly important area of child abuse practice, family supports such as day care and home-maker services have been curtailed.

The severe pressure on public sector spending is, of course, familiar to social workers in most welfare state countries. In Britian the fiscal squeeze has been accompanied by a dramatic rightward shift in the ideological climate and a fierce attack on welfare state services. This has put welfare workers in a precarious position and set the stage for their scapegoating, which, in turn has been fueled by the well publicized deaths of children who were active cases of social service departments. The Maria Colwell case in 1974 was the first and most infamous. Following her death an official inquiry essentially put an individual social worker on public trial (Davies 1985). The media fanned and sustained the panic and public reaction was so heated that Maria's social worker had to be assigned a bodyguard to escort her in and out of the inquiry building (Shearer 1979). Following Colwell, a number of other scandals and reports kept the issue before the public. Since Colwell, there have been at least twenty-five separate inquires into failures in handling child abuse cases in Britain (*Manchester Guardian Weekly* 1987). The result was a climate of enormous anxiety in social service departments so that a 1978 government research report characterized social workers' feelings concerning their relationship to their communities as quite simply one of fear (Parsloe and Stevenson 1978). These events set the stage for my study of British social work practice in child abuse. Now I want to turn to the theoretical debates about state welfare and briefly outline the major points of the theoretical positions I address. I will then present some of the empirical data on which I base my analysis, and finally I will summarize my critique of deterministic left analyses.

Theoretical Explanations of Contemporary State Social Work

How have theorists explained these developments in the organization and practice of state social work? Within the left, one explanation has concentrated on the labour process of state welfare workers. This has involved borrowing the Marxist concept of proletarianization. Harry Braverman did much to popularize this view in his 1974 publication of *Labour and Monopoly Capital: The Degradation of Work in the Twentieth Century*. Braverman's basic premise is that the capitalist labour process is dominated and shaped by the drive for capital accumulation. Degradation of work results from two central imperatives of the capitalist labour process—the concern to cheapen labour, and the need to guarantee effective capitalist control over the production process. Application of the principles of scientific management, Braverman states, involves a process of continuous subdivision and reorganization of the work process to bring it under effective managerial control. The fractionalization and routinization of work results in a steady decline in the skills, knowledge and responsibilities of most workers. The prototypical victim of this deskilling process is the assembly line worker. In the context of recent changes in the organization of social services, some Marxist theorists argued that the thesis of proletarianization could be applied to state welfare occupations like social work. Organization and control over the labour process of public sector workers, they argue, mirror the capitalist labour process of the productive sphere.

Application of the Proletarianization Thesis to State Social Work

Nick Frost (1977), for example, contends that many of the features of the capitalist labour process have now been reproduced within the social work labour process. The hypothesis is that the daily practice of social workers is now under direct managerial control and is subject to the same process of routinization and subdivision as Braverman described for assembly line workers. Individual worker autonomy is no longer then a characteristic of social work practice in state agencies. Following Braverman, Frost analyzes the trend towards centralization of management control within social service structures in terms of the scientific management principles of Taylor. Within this framework, it is postulated that control over the labour process is sought through the separation of "conception from execution" of tasks. Further, it is argued, planning and coordinating functions (i.e., conception) are increasingly controlled by a small number of senior managers and administrators. The performance (execution) of tasks is then carried out by front-line field workers. This concurs with Braverman's analysis that the "overall purpose of all administrative control is, as in the case of production controls, the illumination of uncertainty and the exercise of constraint to achieve the desired result" (Braverman 1974: 265).

However, within social work the basis for technical control is limited because of the unpredictable and unique nature of the input (clients), and the basis of social work production in specific skills largely employed in face-to-face contact with clients beyond management scrutiny. Social workers are thus not subject to direct monitoring;

management must rely on indirect means through administrative procedures and its control of resources to shape practitioners' options.

At the same time, since labour costs do represent a major portion of local authority spending, Frost maintains that control over the labour process of state workers is necessary to improve the productivity of social welfare organizations. He argues that management efforts are directed toward increasing the rate of exploitation of state workers and further through a subdivision of social work activity into separate tasks which may then be performed by cheaper units of labour such as social work assistants. These processes, Frost argues, combine to produce a tendency toward deskilling social work practice and proletarianization of the social worker (Frost, 1977).

Braverman identified this as "the disassociation of the labour process from the skills of the worker, the labour process must be rendered independent of craft, tradition, and workers' knowledge"(*op. cit.* 1974: 118). In this process, once management's monopoly over knowledge of the production process is complete, each step of the labour process and its execution can then be controlled. In social work we would expect it to be reflected in a trend toward increasing separation between control over policy planning and development and its execution in practice. However, perhaps because the basis of service delivery is through individual social workers to individual clients, this latter state of total management monopoly becomes difficult to envisage.

Immediate control over her/his labour process is maintained by the social worker precisely because much social work practice is composed of direct face-to-face interaction between the worker and client(s), often outside the agency. Direct monitoring is therefore not feasible; rather, control must be exercised indirectly through coordination of resources, and conformity to bureaucratic norms, such as quantitative analysis of output and obligatory recording and filing activity reports on practice.

Critique of Deskilling Thesis in Relation to Social Work Practice

Can this form of management control in social work be compared to control over the capitalist labour process sought through Taylor's scientific management? As we have seen, some theorists believe that these tendencies are now apparent in the social work labour process. These tendencies are perhaps most advanced in the area of statutory work, such as child abuse, which has been an area of social work practice subject to external control and increased management intervention. However, it is clear that this analysis of the capitalist labour process cannot be mechanically applied to social work since the latter is a process under the control of the State. The State is a political apparatus. Its form is subject to, amongst other things, the prevailing balance of class forces; thus, changes in the organization of state social work cannot be explained as a directly economic occurrence subject in the same way, as Braverman tried to explain the capitalist labour process (Frost 1977).

Given the difficulty of direct monitoring of welfare labour processes, it would be expected that a certain level of discretion remains with front-line workers. Further, given the nature of human predicaments being presented to social service departments, the possibility of such standardization of practice seems remote even if it were thought desirable. My research, which I will summarize briefly, indicates that a straightforward thesis of proletarianization is problematic when applied to state welfare practice (Davies 1985).

Braverman's analysis of deskilling, while it makes a contribution to understanding tendencies towards increasing managerial control in state bureaucracies, is overly deterministic when applied to the practice of social work. As the qualitative data will show this theoretical approach fails to address the contradictory nature of social work practice, particularly apparent in statutory practice, where both care and control objectives simultaneously exist. For example, for social workers in child welfare a major source of disquiet stems from their power to remove children against their will and against their parents will. Social workers are called upon to build caring and close relationships with children and their parents while at the same time they know they may have to exercise their statutory powers to break up families. Opposing objectives of both 'care' and 'control' exist simultaneously in child welfare (Satyamurti 1979, Bolger 1981). These conflicting elements are central to the day to day experience of social work practice yet are unaccounted for in Braverman's approach.

Braverman's theoretical explanation of changes in the labour process rests at an economic level in terms of increased capital accumulation. However, to adequately address the position of state workers in a non-capitalist sector, it is recognized as necessary to include an analysis of the ideological and political sphere as well. Professions associated with ideological reproduction, as Heraud notes, "do not necessarily respond to the direct dictates of the central mechanisms of capitalism, thus between the state and the professions there are discontinuities and areas of autonomy that preclude a rigidly deterministic model" (1978: 19). This analysis does not concur with Braverman's thesis, since he did not address such complexities in his analysis of labour process determinants. This emphasizes the weakness of a purely economistic analysis in understanding the organization of public sector occupations. The economism of Marxist labour process theories leads to an overemphasis on production relations, and thus hinders an exploration of the relationship between change in the organization of social work and wider political and social antagonisms beyond the point of production.

Ideological Explanation of the Organization of State Social Work

A competing theoretical explanation of the present organization of state welfare services focuses on their ideological importance in the reproduction of the social relations of capitalism. The variant of this theoretical approach which I am concerned with here is that which stresses the social control functions of the welfare State and its agents. I will try to show that this critique represents a form of ideological determinism which presents a distorted view of social workers and clients' experience.

Within this theoretical view, recent changes in the organization and practice of welfare is linked to a rightward shift in the ideological climate noticeable in many western countries. An appreciation of the connection between economic and ideological factors is crucial to understanding the threat posed to social-democratic ideas and practice during a period of crisis for capitalism. Such a period, it is thought makes possible a radical shift in the ideological climate. Hall (1978) and others focusing on the British case (Gamble 1982, 1983; Simpkin 1979; Cockburn 1977, etc.) believe that social democracy has now collapsed in Thatcherite Britain. The ascendancy of the New Right's monetarist economic policies and anti-welfare state social policies, they claim, has firmly swept away the old social-democratic order. Hall believes this has now been replaced by a new consensus based on law and order (1978) which has taken hold as the crisis of capital has deepened. The impact of the New Right is seen not only in harsh economic policies, but also in social policies and the new politics of welfare.

This thesis of the law-and-order State has been advanced by Stuart Hall (1978) and others. This theoretical position at an ideological level is similar to Braverman's approach to the economic level in that the notion of 'control' over the working class is central. In order to theoretically situate the relationship of a changed ideological climate to the labour process of state welfare workers, we will consider Nigel Parton's (1981) application of Hall's thesis of moral panic to the issue of child abuse.

Rise of the New Right

The crisis of capital, Hall and others contend, has led to a right-wing ideological shift. Proponents of the New Right argue for the freeing up of market forces and concomitant reduction and reshaping of the public sector. Theorists of New Right economics and social policies point out:

> At the heart of the Tory approach to the welfare state is the assumption that the market is the most efficient allocator of resources. Conversely, it is argued that the welfare state stifles individual initiative and limits "freedom."...So...the frontiers of the welfare state must be rolled back to make room for more capitalist enterprise and individual self-help.
>
> The guise under which this classic laissez-faire aversion to state welfare has passed in recent years is the apparently apolitical notion of efficiency. Thus, the government has asserted frequently that public expenditure must be cut back because it lies at the heart of Britain's economic difficulties and that there is no alternative... (Walker 1984: 50).

From the premise of an economic crisis, Hall and others are concerned to elucidate the ideological response to this crisis and the entrenchment of a law-and-order State or disciplinary state in Britain. This is fully elaborated in *Policing the Crisis: Mugging, The State and Law and Order* (1978). Of particular relevance to my research focus is their use of the concept of "moral panic" and their analysis of the role of such panics in securing a new ideological consensus. The term "moral panic" was originated by S. Cohen, who claimed that:

> Societies appear to be subject every now and then to periods of moral panic. A condition, episode, person, or group of persons emerges to become defined as a threat to societal values and interests...Sometimes the object of the panic is quite novel and at other times it is something which has been in existence long enough but suddenly appears in the limelight (Cohen 1973: 1).

Moral panics are signified when the reaction to a perceived threat is out of all proportion to its actual existence. Successful moral panics define the boundaries of concern within the dominant ideology and are critical in legitimizing unusual state intervention. Hall argues that moral panics are one of the principle forms by which a silent majority is won over to the support of increasingly coercive measures on the part of the State (Hall *et al.*, 1978).

Moral Panic and Child Abuse

Parton (1981) uses the concept of moral panic to analyze the reaction to child abuse during the mid-seventies in Britain. Starting from the premise that child abuse has existed in some form throughout history, Parton wants to explain how and why it came to be identified as a specific social problem, requiring active state intervention, in the early seventies. He inserts this process of "discovery" and consolidation of child abuse as a problem within a larger context of changes in "material conditions and ideological forces" in British society.

The Maria Colwell inquiry in 1974 and subsequent series of child abuse tragedies precipitated an unprecedented attack on social work and scapegoating of social workers. Parton argues that the reaction to these events can be characterized as "moral panic" and links the events in statutory child welfare practice in the mid-seventies to the increasing dominance of the New Right. The child abuse panic, Parton believes, produced a climate favourable for management to "consolidate administrative and managerial procedures in the new social service departments" (1979: 441). This process of management consolidation is linked by Bolger *et al.*, (1981) to other developments in the restructuring of the State and cutbacks in health and social services and education, which is, in turn, related to the restructuring of capital engendered by the economic crisis.

After the Maria Colwell tragedy, Parton and others argue, a coercive shift in the social work role occurred. Social service departments, anxious to avoid similar incidents, have become "more overtly controlling, potentially more punitive, and act as adversary as often as helper" (Packman 1981: 127) in dealing with families. Thus Parton argues that the "rise of the new right", represented by the phenomenon of Thatcherism in England, has a direct relationship to the practice of social work within welfare state structures. Parton believes that social workers have thus been pushed into a coercive and intrusive practice, particularly in child abuse work.

The social work role is increasingly one of policing deviant families. Following this theoretical position, it would not be coincidental that such a reorientation of welfare practice would occur within the context of an economic crisis and subsequent shake-up of capital. Such a context creates for the State an increased need for domestic stability. The experience of economic crisis heightens the need for state supports and underwriting of families' caring functions, yet the reduction of the public sector simultaneously denies this possibility. Families must therefore be disciplined to 'manage' on their own; those who fail to do so are subject to coercive state intervention.

Within this optic, the example of the moral panic around child abuse could be seen as a vehicle for heightened management control over statutory practice of state social workers. Such management control is consistent with the postulated tendency to centralize state operations in advanced capitalist States. Management control over the labour process of welfare workers would be crucial to this process.

In the optic of these theorists, then, it is argued that the climate of insecurity in social service departments created by the child abuse panic facilitated the assertion of management control and the reshaping of social relations within the organization of state social work.

Linda Davies

Weakness of Thesis Approaches in Relation to State Welfare Work

The thesis of ideological determinism (Hall *et al.*, 1978; Parton 1981) is consistent with Braverman's (1974) thesis of economic determinism in that they both advance the notion that control is central. In Braverman's case, he is concerned with capital's control over the labour process in production settings, while Hall and Parton are concerned with the State's reassertion of ideological control in a period of hegemonic crisis. These different perspectives, economic and ideological, have some resonance within the current context of social services.

The shift toward hierarchical control in state welfare structures is evident. The panic around child abuse has clearly contributed to a climate of anxiety in social service departments. Yet while it is clear that general economic and political conditions exert significant constraints, it is not clear that the organization of social work and its practice are successfully 'determined' by such conditions. Similarly, the shift in the ideological context does not necessarily have direct and uniform consequences on the delivery of services at the front line.

The overly simple view of these approaches posits a picture of total and successful control of both welfare workers and their working-class clients. It is my contention that neither deskilling nor simple social control theories adequately account for important aspects of practitioners' experience of child abuse practice. Nor do other social divisions around which social welfare is constructed receive any attention in these analyses. For example, client families are depicted as homogenous units sucessfully controlled by state agents. As will be discussed later, gender and age divisions within the family are simply not addressed.

A Study of British Child Abuse Practice

To illustrate my case I will draw on empirical research on English social workers' experience of child abuse practice. There are some marked differences in the organizational structure of social work in Britain. Social work is both more decentralized and more directly accountable politically. Social workers are employed by local boroughs which may be controlled by the Labour or Conservative parties. In the inner London borough where I did this study, a left Labour council was in power and the borough had been Labour-controlled for years. Although legislation governing child protection is national and the Department of Health and Social Security sets national guidelines for practice, considerable variation exists between boroughs in terms of ideology and level of resources available.

In my borough, social workers were employed in ten geographic teams of ten to fifteen workers each. Each team was comprised of a team leader, a few supervisors and several front-line workers as well as administrative and clerical staff. In one area where I conducted interviews, the team used a peer supervision model which involved the whole team in case discussions. The other team I studied used a more traditional one-to-one supervision model. The research relied on content analysis of qualitative data from interviews with sixteen local authority social workers. These workers were all qualified social workers, but at varying length of experience. Included among the sixteen interviewees were four supervisors (or seniors as the British call them) and two team leaders. Apart from the two team leaders, all interviewed social workers were directly involved in statutory cases of non-accidental injury or child abuse.

A major concern of my inquiry was workers' experience with, and use of, the child abuse manual of procedures on how to conduct a child abuse case. This dimension of the study is related directly to the proletarianization thesis, whose proponents would view such management initiated procedures as examples of successful bureaucratic control over practice. My interviews showed that management control is not as pervasive as the proletarianization thesis would suggest, and further, that there are limits to this kind of control which are inherent in social work practice.

It was not uncommon for workers to be unaware of management initiated structures and procedures. Some had not even read the child abuse manual! Indeed, even awareness of its existence did not ensure familiarity with the content. If workers can remain oblivious to the existence of structures and procedures which are meant to guide their practice, it is difficult to argue they have lost their autonomy.

For some other workers however, the very existence of a manual of procedures generated anxiety and guilt when they tried in vain to make their cases conform to official rules. The chaotic reality of case developments and events often were at odds with the linear steps and categories laid out in the manual. Although management attempted to impose formal instructions for handling child abuse cases, the manual did not always or usually have obvious day to day relevance.

When they were aware of formal procedures, workers had to use considerable judgement to interpret the rules in daily practice. For example, the decision to put a child's name on the abuse register depends on a worker's assessment of risk. The rule stipulates that children should be registered in cases of "grave professional concern" but obviously this is subject to interpretation; the detailed basis for such decisions cannot be spelled out in advance. Rather, each decision requires subjective, on the spot interpretation. As one team leader said,

> However much you try to standardize a procedure, people's judgement about where that procedure is applicable will always vary and some people philosophically will do their best to keep everybody off the register and some people will say that everybody ought to be on the register. Some people will just forget to take them off and so it isn't a foolproof way of making sure that that is the hard core of real problems at all.

An important point to remember about child abuse work is that despite media sensationalization of dramatic cases, most are not clear cut as to the degree of risk; the vast majority are borderline or grey area cases. Every judgement courts risk. Social workers cannot always whisk children away for their own protection or remove children on the slightest suspicion because to do so would undermine any potential for on-going work with families.

This is illustrated in the decision to involve the court in a child abuse case. In such instances, the unpredictable support of courts for social work requests in such cases heightens uncertainty; therefore workers must exercise discretion as to when or if to take this step. In the words of a front-line worker,

> It is a calculated risk to place a kid back at home that has been battered, but it's a worse risk in my opinion to go to court and ask for a care order when you are not certain you are going to get one because you may have really blown the

> thing wide apart by then and you may be risking somebody's life. It's very difficult...

So there is not necessarily a direct relationship between a set of rules and practitioner's behavior. Workers may ignore, adapt or change the rules as their judgement suggests. Despite management's procedures and structures, child abuse practice contains elements of uncertainty and discretion. There are barriers or limits to the strict application of procedures. Even in statutory work, a practice that is 'determined' from above cannot exist; social workers cannot simply follow rules. Yet, given the intense anxiety which now surrounds child abuse practice, workers experience this discretion as highly uncomfortable.

> You're anxious because if the kid dies, or is horribly maimed and you've been going into that family, you're the one who's going to get the blame. There's very much the tension about the situation that if you make a mistake, and you're quite likely to make a mistake, it's going to be your fault.

In the face of this, some workers, aware of the child abuse manual, are tempted to 'cover themselves' through strict conformity with all bureaucratic procedures, or further try to reduce risk to themselves by overcautious clinical decision-making. For example, some workers leave a child's name on the child abuse register to protect themselves rather than because the clinical situation strictly warrants it.

> Well, it's just easier to leave them on, because if anything goes wrong and you've taken them off the register, you stand a sort of culprit, you haven't done your work properly.

Often, adherence to procedure has not so much to do with workers' judgement of clinical risk as with their fears. Formal procedures and structures can be experienced as necessary supports in that they provide to some degree a guide to prudent action and a defense against public criticism.

> It's such a sensitive and highly explosive area, I think it made me feel a lot safer to know we've actually got a

> guideline, so if anything goes wrong, you can say, look we've got a guideline, this is what we're going by, whereas if you were all by yourself as a social worker, on your own initiative, making your own decisions...I'm really glad there is a guideline.

In summary, welfare practitioners maintain significant autonomy within their labour process. Even in the highly prescribed area of child abuse practice, workers have discretion whether they want it or not. Despite a proliferation of procedures and structures, management control in social work is not as successful as we might be led to believe. Further, it is clear that there are limits to this form of control over what is essentially a 'practice'. It is impossible to completely subject workers' practice to a set of rules and procedures. Social workers' accounts of their cases indicate that such rules and guidelines often are only marginally related to the reality of practice. The intrinsic necessity for judgement and interpretation, even in situations meant to be covered by rules, creates a "margin of manoeuvre" that helps explain why social workers feel responsible for events concerning their clients which are seemingly beyond control. Without such a margin of manoeuvre they would not feel, nor could they be made to feel, in any way anxious or responsible for their clients' welfare. This is in direct contrast to welfare officers, for example, who simply apply pre-determined regulations concerning eligibility. Workers' anxiety about child abuse practice helps us to understand their experience of supervision. This is not analogous to the supervision by the foreman on the factory floor; it is even seen as a potential source of support and protection. This raises another point that needs emphasis: the ambivalence social workers feel about their autonomy. This ambivalence is understandably intensified in a period with arduous and hostile conditions of practice.

The institutions, policies, and practices in child welfare were constructed within a social democratic framework which contains inevitable contradictions. Child welfare legislation, for example, reflects a constant compromise and tension between care and control elements. The contradictory orientations of justice versus welfare (i.e., a judicial versus a rehabilitative or welfare approach) leave workers without clear guidelines to orient their practice. In the area of child abuse practice, social workers are further caught between contradictory ideologies concerning families and children. On the one hand, we think that families are supremely good and that children always belong with their parents, while on the other, we think that children have rights and that we have a responsibility to protect them.

The family continues as both haven and locus of oppression, and the contradictory state policies toward the family continue under radical right politics, such as Thatcherism, despite pressure on resources and ideological attacks on the welfare State. Social workers' practice takes place within these contradictions. We should thus not be surprised that being a social worker is also experienced as highly contradictory and that exercising discretion is perceived as highly uncomfortable and sometimes even dangerous.

The profession's claims to be able to do something about child abuse and workers' feeling that they ought to be able to 'help' are consistent with a social-democratic ideology and response to social problems. Despite the structural conditions that give rise to this and other social problems, the therapeutic casework model continues to be dominant. Welfare workers and their clients continue, therefore, to have an individualized experience of welfare institutions and practice

The emotional anxiety and stress in child abuse work must be understood in this context. Understandably, social workers are looking for guidance and direction. However, they were not satisfied with management initiatives in the area of child abuse; in particular, these were characterized as both too distant and too bureaucratic. Rather, management structures are only indirectly related to the disorder and confusion of day-to-day practice. Although social service management may be trying to exert some control over child abuse practice and to diminish individual autonomy, and while workers may actually desire this, discretion remains. Given this, social work theorists need to take into account workers' needs for both structure and control, while also recognizing the necessity for workers to act.

Theoretical Implications and Conclusions

The theoretical starting point for my research was an attempt to elaborate Braverman's theory of the capitalist labour process by applying it to state welfare work. However, it became apparent to me in the course of this study that Braverman's thesis could not be supported in relation to state welfare, as the tenets of the proletarianization thesis were not evident in the empirical data. Further, Braverman's whole theoretical approach simply could not cope with the understanding of welfare labour processes that the interview data were generating. These issues suggest that we reappraise what theory and methods are necessary to understand state labour processes and welfare practices.

Braverman's thesis can be criticized in its own terms because of the primacy he gives to capital in shaping the labour process. The labour process is not conceived as a terrain of active class struggle, but rather represents a battle already won by capital through an inexorable process of deskilling labour. This reflects a non-dialectical understanding of how labour processes are constructed. Braverman neglected worker resistance as a force in shaping the process of production, nor did he address contradictions around gender and their impact on the labour process. For example, feminists have pointed out that businessmen may present obstacles to clerical proletarianization because they want the status and individual attention that personal secretaries provide. Therefore, ideological and gendered divisions may not conform to an economistic analysis of the labour process.

The Braverman type of analysis has been criticized by other Marxist theorists as determinist and top-down because of its *a priori* assumptions about the capital accumulation process. Moreover, these labour process theories result in an exclusive emphasis on production relations, and thus limit an exploration of the relationship between changes in labour processes and wider political and social antagonisms beyond the point of production. Such an understanding is crucial to the intelligibility of state social work.

In attempting to apply a capital determined labour process theory to an analysis of changes in the organization of work in the state sector, we must ask a central question: Of what significance for the shaping of labour processes is the fact that these are constructed within the state human service sector? To analyze simply by analogy is to retain an economism which privileges a functional relationship to the capital accumulation process. The focus is simply extended to identifying conditions in the State which might give rise to a fiscal crisis, and therefore a theoretical rationale on economic grounds for the proletarianization of state workers. This obscures the obvious importance of ideological contradictions and tensions in relation to welfare work.

The Braverman explanation doesn't readily fit occupations where workers have a commitment to the outcome of their labour process. Social workers get involved, emotional and burnt out. The central antagonism between capital and labour perhaps does not exist in the same way within welfare work as it does elsewhere. The commitment social workers feel may well stem from bourgeois liberal professional ideologies (i.e., the service ethic) but some alternative socialist ideologies would also embrace this commitment. Given that theories of the labour process historically have concerned men and men's work, we should perhaps expect that these theories encounter problems when applied to an arena of social reproduction which has historically concerned women.

'Women's work' in social care roles cannot be theorized in the same way that we theorize the production of cars. Yet 'women's work' in social reproduction generally is absent as a category of analysis within labour process theories. Male analyses of 'labour' traditionally have understood this category within male terms (i.e., as involving 'male work' which is paid labour). Thus, paid labour has been treated as a major, important activity, and therefore has been the object of much theoretical analysis.

In the area of welfare and related culturally female work, the recent theoretical contributions concerning social care giving activity is promising. 'Care' as a category cuts across the traditional conceptual divisions and can include paid labour, unpaid domestic labour, and love or 'duty'.

It is possible that in understanding what welfare work is about, the category of work alone is not theoretically helpful. Graham (1983) argues that "caring" is a social relationship that cannot be understood objectively and abstractly, but only as a subjective experience and that further, the gendered nature of caring needs to be confronted. Institutions of caring—the family, the community and the State—are social structures which contain class, race and gender relations and these need to be the subject of specific analyses.

I have also taken issue with theoretical approaches which see welfare work simply as social control; for example, Parton's analysis of a coercive shift in welfare practice, which he links to broad rightward ideological shifts. The concepts of policing and social control, while seductive, approach non-explanation and incoherence under sustained scrutiny. As Stedman Jones (1977) has noted, the problem is a conceptual one in that the theoretical antecedents of these terms are found within a functionalist Marxism. While these theoretical approaches remain characteristic of much of the left's analysis of welfare, it is politically important to debate their claims.

Linda Gordon, writing within a feminist perspective, has analyzed the shortcomings of what she terms "simple social control" critiques. First, she points out that the condemnation of social control, and specifically social work intervention into the family as automatically evil, rests on an assumption that there can be such a thing as an autonomous family immune from social regulation. This, she argues, has no historical precedent. Simple social control critiques also imply that clients' problems are not real but simply the result of social workers' biases. Gordon notes that these explanations usually see the flow of initiative from top to bottom (i.e., from managers to workers, from social workers to clients). This depicts the objects of social control efforts as powerless victims. Her work shows, on the contrary, that clients are not simply passive victims but frequently initiated social work intervention themselves and with their own agendas in mind. This is often not recognized in social control critiques because they conceive of the family as a homogeneous unit unmarked by gender and age divisions. Yet Gordon argues that the outcome of social work intervention, however unintended, was often a challenge to male authority within the family. This is particularly evident in present practice in the area of sexual abuse (Gordon 1985; Mitchell and Oakley 1986). Explanations which concentrate on social control in terms of class can leave unaddressed other forms of domination such as that between men and women and between adults and children. Gordon calls for the development of an adequate feminist theory of social control because, of course, feminist theorists are not immune from the criticisms she makes. Indeed, some feminist analyses reproduce a crude determinism by simply substituting gender for class.

To understand state welfare work we need theoretical approaches which can provide the tools to adequately theorize contradictions and politics around, for example, gender relations, the family, parenting and other social care relations. This suggests the importance of recent contributions made by feminist welfare theorists who call attention to the necessity of expanding our understanding of the gendered nature of welfare state structures and practice. Feminists theorists (Wilson 1977; Voigt 1986; Brook and Davis 1985) argue that without an analysis of patriarchy it is impossible to comprehend the workings of the welfare

State. They highlight the predominance of women in the field of welfare as both givers and receivers of service. Such analyses examine the consequences for women of the bureaucratization of social work and draw attention to the division of labour within social work which mirrors the position of women in other occupations in which men fill a disproportionate share of managerial posts while women dominate the front line. A parallel process of devaluation of expressive qualities in the social work client relation and in the larger organization is characteristic of the present bureaucratic structure. Feminist theorists are attempting to come to grips with the complex interrelationships between patriarchy, the family, and the organization of state welfare. The importance of feminist analysis lies in its potential to address the dialectical relationships between social structures and individual experience. State welfare workers' feelings of powerlessness can be challenged through analyses which stress the contradictions in welfare structures and encourage exploitation of the margin of manoeuvre that exists. To combat "crippling fatalism" our theoretical understanding of welfare work needs to both reflect its complexity and dilemmas, and have sufficient practical implications to be useful to workers seeking an alternative form of practice within state welfare structures.

NOTES

1. A shorter version of this appears in the *Canadian Review on Social Policy*, 25, 1990.

Chapter Four

THE INUIT COMMUNITY WORKERS' EXPERIENCE OF YOUTH PROTECTION WORK

Laura Mastronardi

This essay analyzes the experience of Inuit community workers employed by the Québec State to implement its youth protection mandate in the remote northern settlements of Ungava Bay. The hiring of Inuit by the Social Service Centre to work in the area of statutory child welfare began in the early 1980s. Previously, whites had been employed to do this work, and the change in hiring practice was prompted by conditions of the James Bay Northern Québec Agreement signed in 1975[1] and later, by the implementation of the Youth Protection Act in 1979. While the presence of indigenous workers in the service organization acknowledges the need to increase Native participation in the delivery of social services, the current context of statutory practice constrains the nature and extent of their participation. While Inuit have become more politically involved in the administration of their own affairs, white administrators' insistence on the correctness of their own institutional rules serves to keep the Inuit down (Paine 1977: 105-131). The consequences of this arrangement are felt keenly by indigenous workers in their day-to-day youth protection work.

Relying on interviews with Inuit community workers and field observation of their practice, this paper will analyze how the conditions for youth protection work in the north, as experienced by the workers, encourage their passive subordination to the bureaucratic organization of practice. This tendency emerges in response to the impossible situations in which workers find themselves as they try to conform to the requirements of the law and, at the same time, to the norms and realities of Inuit village life. Their passive subordination to the administrative apparatus is best understood as a strategy for coping with seemingly unresolvable practice dilemmas. While this strategy is a reasonable means by which to manage the demands of the job from day to day, it does little to further the conceptual and practical development of an Inuit approach to youth protection work. By situating the workers' accounts of their practice experience within the organizational, legislative and community contexts in which it occurs, we can begin to identify some of obstacles which impede their efforts to define their mandate in practice.

I begin by exploring the Inuit workers' experience of subordination as a consequence of their structural location in the social service bureaucracy and their ethnic minority status. The community workers' sense of subordination to the administrative apparatus has a pervasive influence on their practice experience. While certain structures within the service organization offer workers some measure of support and protection with respect to their case decisions, the very nature of this support urges conformity to the bureaucratic organization of the work (Davies 1985).

The legislative and policy framework of child welfare services largely determines the form and content of youth protection work. I will examine the community workers' experience of this framework, revealing how the foreign auspice of their mandate is problematic in several respects. Most essentially, the lack of legitimacy accorded the "white man's law" in the north deprives workers of a clear sanction for their role and practice. The sanction available to workers thus resides within the bureaucracy and their compliance to administrative expectations of their work.

The Inuit workers' attempts to satisfy the requirements of the law, subject to bureaucratic norms of public administration, in a setting where the norms and realities of village life militate against such conformity, sets up a fundamental tension in their experience of day-to-day practice. This tension is exacerbated by the workers' close identification with their communities. Therefore, I will examine how the local conditions of work require that community workers define and implement the law in a culturally sensitive way while, simultaneously, making it difficult for them to develop practice norms.

I will also consider the Inuit workers' socialization to the profession of social work to see how the nature and outcomes of this process function to sustain rather than mitigate the conflicts and tensions they experience in daily practice. The lack of legitimation and professional identity that result from the Inuit workers' weak professionalization limits their capacity to resist the administrative definition of their work.

Despite the many constraints on their youth protection work, the community workers are active agents in the construction of their own practice experience. The empirical evidence suggests that they are making some progress, albeit limited to date, to develop a distinctive indigenous approach to statutory practice. With this in mind, I will conclude with a brief consideration of the future of youth protection work in the north.

The community workers whose experience is analyzed in this essay are not professionally accredited social workers and have had varying lengths of experience in youth protection work. With the exception of those workers located at the Social Service Centre regional office in Kuujjuak, they practice alone in their respective communities where they are employed on a part-time basis.

A crucial feature of social work practice in the north is that community workers carry responsibilty for several mandates: the Youth Protection Act, Young Offender's Act, and the coordination of home care under the Health Services Act. The combined requirements of the job place excessive demands on individual workers, many of whom remain unsure of the limits of their authority and responsibility with respect to any one mandate.

The observations of community worker practice cited and analyzed herein derive from a two month field study conducted in two Inuit settlements on the Ungava Bay coast. Data were gathered through unstructured, indepth interviews with the workers, and participant-observation of their day-to-day practice and of a two week training session involving workers from both Hudson and Ungava Bay coasts. The community workers in the two settlements were actively involved in the initial analysis of the data, a process which enabled me to focus on the conditions of work which they identified as most influential in shaping their practice experience.

COMMUNITY WORKERS' EXPERIENCE OF SUBORDINATION

Social Work Practice Within State Bureaucracy

The recommendations of the Castonguay commission in the early seventies prompted a massive restructuring of the organizational context of social work practice in Québec. The State's efforts to maximize the efficiency and cost effectiveness of its welfare apparatus, along with a technocratic vision, resulted in a highly centralized state bureaucracy.[2] These developments have had far-reaching consequences for both social workers and clients. The status and role of professionals has been greatly diminished by the predominance of managerial authority and the extensive division of labour which leaves those engaged in direct service delivery with little say in the planning and coordination of services (Davies, Thomsom 1983: 14). The consolidation of decision-making authority in the highest echelons leaves social workers feeling powerless in the face of the administrative hierarchy. The further devaluation of direct practice through the higher pay and status of administrators and the lack of career paths for clinicians adds to the frustration and disenchantment with 'the system' that are common sentiments among front-line workers.

The severe pressure on public expenditures since the mid-seventies has limited the quality and availability of resources that workers can offer to clients. Confronted by serious constraints on resources, social workers are having to resort to a more controlling relationship with their clients. Some analysts have argued that in youth protection work the practice emphasis is now on disciplining families to manage on their own or be subject to coercive and punitive state intervention (i.e., removal of a child).[3]

The push on workers to 'get tough' with clients does not arise from economic considerations alone. Attacks on social work itself, precipitated by the moral panic around child abuse[4] and charges of how the youth protection system has failed,[5] have prompted managers of social service departments to step up their efforts to monitor front-line practice. The pressure on social workers to comply with the bureaucratic organization of practice is considerable given the high-risk nature of child abuse cases in particular. However, even in youth protection, which is perhaps the most highly regulated and tightly structured form of social work practice, workers retain some measure of discretion in their day-to-day work. However, in the current climate, this discretion often is perceived by social workers as a dangerous thing (Davies 1985).

While clients occupy the most starkly dependent role in relation to organizations and their resources, social workers too occupy a subordinate position within the state bureaucracy. However, if we hope to appreciate the situation of indigenous community workers, we must also recognize the sense of subordination that accrues from their cultural identity as Inuit.

The Impact of Institutionalized Racism[6]

The community workers' position within the social service structure parallels that of Inuit in the broader social, economic and political context of Canadian society where, as members of a minority ethnic group, they are discriminated against in their efforts to participate fully in the institutions of the dominant society.[7] Community workers labour under a dual sense of subordination, first as state agents constrained by the social and bureaucratic context of their work and secondly, as a direct consequence of their cultural identity. Although the hiring of Inuit workers by the social service agency may suggest a shift away from the paternalistic model of ethnic relations[8] that has characterized the historical relationship between Inuit and the State, the current administration remains nonetheless colonial. The community workers' relationship to the bureaucracy continues to be shaped by white tutelage.[9] As one worker observed:

> They [white administrators] might be very nice to us because we can help them to get things done. They don't speak Inuktitut so they need our help. But sometimes I think that they take advantage of us. Maybe they think that we Inuit are dumb or something.

The suggestion that community workers feel taken advantage of by the agency, and that perhaps administrators do not recognize that workers have this perception of their relationship to the organization, reveals the extent to which the tutelage complex remains intact. In their interaction with the social service bureaucracy, Inuit workers find themselves placed in a childlike role; those who conform to the tutor's norms of public administration will be rewarded, but when there is deviation from what the tutors deem appropriate, support may be withdrawn. The community workers' dependance upon the agency for the resources with which to do their job maintains this arrangement.

The Inuit workers' accounts of their practice suggest that they have to some extent accepted their denigration and collude with the process of their own domination even as they resist it. This process manifests itself in their interactions with other professionals in the village (i.e., nurses, police constables and teachers), the majority of whom are white southerners. There is a pronounced tendency for the community workers to defer to other professionals, even when doing so is likely to jeopardize their own interventions. The following, in which a female worker recalls her involvement in a presumably joint investigation of sexual abuse, illustrates this point.

> Researcher: Before going to the school, did you have any opportunity to talk with the police about how the two of you [community worker and police constable] would do the investigation?
>
> Worker: No. I didn't know what to do. I thought that all these police had good experience in these cases, so I followed him, but he did not do a good job. Do you mean that it would be okay for me to tell the police how I think we should do the investigation?

Although the worker's decision to comply with the constable's plan for the investigation was prompted in part by her own lack of knowledge, there were clearly other factors at work. As an Inuk woman, she did not see herself as an equal partner in a joint investigation with a white, male police officer. An experienced female worker recalls her frustration in dealing with a police constable in a case of alleged sexual abuse:

> He would not agree to let me go and interview the child on my own. I explained why I felt this was a good idea, but he said no, I was along to interpret. I don't think he believed that I could do a good job. But he didn't find out anything because

the little girl was too afraid to talk to him. On the way back he
gave me a hard time because things didn't go well.

Here again, the community worker complied with the constable's expectations, although in this instance, the worker did try to assert her own views on how best to handle the investigation. However, she did not defend herself against the constable's imputation that she was to blame for the poor outcome of the interview.

In further discussion of these and similar instances, workers revealed that they did not follow up with other professionals about their dissatisfaction with the process of the work as they experienced it. Taken together, the interviews suggest that such deference has complex origins. The phenomenon of deference may be interpreted in a number of ways. It may be, for example, a deliberate strategy to avoid confrontation, something their own culture teaches Inuit to do whenever possible.[10] Given the community workers' sense of subordination, deference may be a strategy of impression management (i.e., an attempt to fit their behaviour to what they believe to be others' expectations of them).[11] Alternatively, by deferring to others, community workers may be privately modifying the scope of their own discretion and authority. By imposing restrictions on the scope of their powers, social workers can to some extent free themselves from perceived responsibility for outcomes (Lipsky 1980: 149).

Confronted with the problem of scant resources with which to help clients, community workers may welcome opportunities to limit their discretion in this way as a means of coping with the discrepancy between resources and the demands of the job. But however we interpret examples of deference, one of the unintended consequences for community workers is that clients and village residents come to doubt their competence to do the job.

LEGISLATIVE AND POLICY CONTEXT OF COMMUNITY WORKER PRACTICE

A Mandate for Youth Protection

At the most fundamental level, the question of goals and objectives in social work is problematic.

> It is impossible to take for granted a goal and work towards it. What one views as a problem, what one accepts as a solution to the problem as defined, and what will be regarded as a satisfactory means for arriving at a given solution to a given problem is a matter of debate: it involves options about the kind of lifestyle one is prepared to tolerate, and will differ according to one's position in the social structure, and in particular, the social structure of the welfare enterprise.[12]

This lack of consensus inevitably gives rise to competing and even contradictory objectives in day-to-day practice. Youth protection work is no exception. In child welfare services there is general agreement that children must be protected against threats to their physical and psychological well-being. Yet what exactly do we mean when we talk about protecting a child? How is risk defined, by whom, and what are the most appropriate means by which to ensure a child's safety while simultaneously respecting both the child's and the parents' rights? These basic questions in youth protection are subject to a wide range of interpretations and beliefs. Our own responses to these and related questions are influenced by the prevailing political and ideological climate of a given historical period, as well as our own experiences of family and community in which cultural differences play an important role.

The Québec Youth Protection Act offers social workers only the most general practice guidelines. As a formal statement of government social policy, the Act attends mostly to administrative, legal and procedural arrangements while the underlying principles and goals are left implicit, ambiguous, open to interpretation. To some extent, this ambiguity is bounded in day-to-day practice by the highly regulated and tightly structured nature of statutory work; there are hierarchical lines of accountability, procedure manuals, supervision and case conference structures. However, considerable latitude remains within which youth protection workers must exercise their discretion. While compliance with formal procedures and regulations offers workers some measure of support and protection concerning their decisions, it is impossible for workers simply to orient their practice to bureaucratic exigencies.[13]

The utility of administrative procedures and rules in providing solutions to problems, and in turn directions for practice, is limited by the complexity of clients' problems. Formalized procedures assume that events unfold clearly and predictably and are amenable therefore to simple, programmatic intervention (Glastonbury et al.,1980: 99). However, in youth protection work the majority of cases fall into a 'grey area' in which current and future risk to the child is unclear. In short, it is difficult for workers to decide whether a child is at sufficient risk to warrant court-ordered supervision or removal from the home (Davies 1985). Ultimately, protective services workers must rely upon their best assessments of fluid situations.

An Inuit worker aptly conveyed how the problem of exercising discretion confronts all youth protection workers.

> The law tells us when we should go to investigate to see if a child is maybe in danger. And the law says that if I think that it is too dangerous for a child to stay with her parents that I should take the child away to a foster home, or to stay with a relative. But I still have to make up my own mind about this. And what if people don't agree with me? Everybody has an opinion.

The diverse opinions surrounding the decision to remove a child renders decision-making even more problematic for front-line workers. Youth protection workers frequently are criticized by clients and the general public for being unnecessarily coercive and intrusive. In the current climate for social work practice, criticism of this nature reflects a major practice dilemma in statutory work. On the one hand, social workers may be accused of being "baby snatchers", while on the other, they may be blamed for failing to adequately protect children from neglectful and abusive caregivers.[14] In effect, workers are caught in a no-win situation so that even the initial decision to intervene may generate considerable anxiety.

Administrative procedures and regulations could not resolve the uncertainty which confronted this new community worker.

> It is sometimes hard to know if we should be involved with a family or if we should stay out. When we know that a child is being neglected or sexually abused, then we don't have to wonder. But sometimes we know that there is a lot of drinking in a home, or maybe that a man beats his wife. In cases like these, we are worried about the kids but it is

> harder to know if we have a right to be there because there is no information to tell us that the children are suffering. Even if we know that it is not good for kids to see their mother beat up. Maybe the mother is not too worried about the children, or maybe she is afraid to tell us anything because she knows that her husband will get back at her.

In cases like this, the lack of 'evidence' concerning the children's status in the home and fear of reprisals by the husband against his wife, and possibly against herself/himself, may provide sufficient reason for the worker to decide not to intervene, or at least not until the situation deteriorates further and there is clearcut evidence of risk to the children. There are few right answers to the tough decisions youth protection workers make in day-to-day practice, and in exercising discretion they court risk to themselves and/or to the child. In this context, the foreign auspice of the Inuit workers' mandate takes on a special significance.

The "White Man's Law"

The Youth Protection Act is commonly referred to in the north, by residents and community workers alike, as the "white man's law". Many Native people regard the legislation with suspicion and scepticism—as another attempt by government to regulate their lives in accordance with dominant society norms. Their concerns are well-founded when we consider that Native interaction with social service institutions in Canadian society has been marked by colonialism and related expressions of racism.[15] As a creation of southern institutions and political processes, the legislation embodies dominant society values and ideologies around parenting. Further, as Gordon notes, standards about what constitutes adequate care of children are inseparable from cultural ideology about proper family life (Gordon 1988: 216). The potential conflicts engendered by such cultural differences have a direct impact on the community workers' practice experience.

Attempts by community workers to implement the youth protection law have earned them the derogatory title of 'policeman'. An experienced male worker explained one of the problems confronting Inuit workers as a consequence of the foreign auspice of their authority.

> It is very hard to accept this, to be called a policeman. I don't like people to think of me this way when I do my job. But people here do not understand that sometimes the law is necessary to protect the child, that some parents will not cooperate without the law. But it used to be that children had to sometimes be taken away from their parents and given to somebody else. I think that people are angry about the law because it is not ours; it comes from outside.

Clearly, the Act is perceived by some Inuit as a coercive form of control imposed by outsiders that serves to displace the self-regulatory practices of traditional Inuit society concerning the care and protection of children. As a result, the law and the community worker role are accorded only minimal legitimacy in the north. When Inuit workers invoke the law as justification for their interventions, they are likely to provoke inordinate resistance from clients as well as criticism from other residents. Moreover, appeals to the law expose workers to accusations of betrayal or selling out in the service of the "white man's law". Under these circumstances, the workers' exercise of authority and discretion is highly problematic.

Role Conflict: Innu as State Agents

The tension that Inuit workers experience in trying to conform to the requirements of the law, and at the same time, to the norms and realities of village life, is heightened by the disjunction between the traditional Inuit conception of the helper's role and the contemporary, bureaucratic definition of the social worker role.

Prior to the implementation of the Youth Protection Act in the north, child protection derived from community self-regulation. Intervention relied upon a consensual process of decision-making and collective action on the part of the family and kinship group. This natural helping network was built from relationships based on equality and reciprocity between those who gave and those who received help, to which, it was believed, each person had a right. The shared responsibility for problem-solving was essential to the integrity and well-being of the group (Brody 1975).

This form of child protection was displaced by the implementation of the Act, which imposed the State's definition and organization of statutory practice and social control. Child protection was reconceptualized as a mandated responsibility to be carried out by state youth protection workers. The Youth Protection Act increased state rationalization of social services and the social control of selected population groups, primarily poor families, single parent (mother led) families, and unemployed youth. Within this legislative framework, social work practice has shifted from a socio-therapeutic to a socio-judicial orientation; i.e., from helping to authority relations with clients (Lesemann, Renaud 1980: 25-51).

Reflecting upon his experience of these changes in his role as helper, one Inuit worker remarked:

> I didn't know that what I was doing all along was social work. But for me, helping people now is harder. Before we didn't have the law and the CSS [Social Service Centre]. If somebody needed help, I would do what I could to support them. But now the law says that I have to help people even when they are not asking for support. It's hard to force somebody to accept help.

Youth protection workers commonly feel uncomfortable when intervening in situations where their help has not been solicited. However, this worker was acknowledging a particular shift in the context of helping, a shift that magnified his discomfort. By virtue of his mandated authority as a state agent, the worker can no longer enjoy the benefits of an egalitarian relationship with the recipient of his services. The altered social relations engendered by the implementation of the Act are troublesome for Inuit workers in part because authority and power accorded on the basis of some *a priori* ascriptive status were not attributes of the traditional helper role.

Attempting a self-portrayal of his emerging identity as a community worker since the implementation of the Act, another individual explained that he is now a helper in the traditional sense of this word (an Inuk who cares about the well-being of others) and a government agent (someone who cares about others because he is legally obligated to do so). The worker's struggle to reconcile these divergent conceptions of his role must be worked out in day-to-day practice where, to satisfy the requirements of the mandate, he may have to violate cultural norms of conduct (i.e., that of non-interference). The crucial adjustment to be made here is for both the worker and client to internalize and act upon the professional and bureaucratic definitions of their roles. They will be rewarded for this, workers by approval from their superiors and clients by positive attention from their worker. Questions of desirability aside, this adjustment cannot come easily, particularly as the inequity inherent in the contemporary definition of the worker-client relationship undermines the traditional Inuit values of equality and reciprocity in helping others.

As state agents, the community workers encounter a major practice dilemma. As long as they strive to comply with administrative expectations of their practice, they are valued by the agency; yet simultaneously their efforts as state agents alienate them from their communities, thereby diminishing their potential value to both the agency and the community (Brody 1975). In this way, the workers come to occupy a marginal position at the interface between the community and the bureaucracy and do not feel a sense of belonging to either one.

This subjective experience of marginality is evident in this worker's reflections.

> Many times I think that nobody understands how we community workers feel. The bosses don't really know how hard it is to use the law here. Maybe they know but don't care because they get upset when we don't do what they want. And the people here don't know about the law and they get angry. Some of them say that we think too much like white men. We are in the middle all the time.

The difficulty of negotiating community and agency is compounded by the youth protection mandate's basis in dominant society ideologies of parenting and family life. Inuit workers have difficulty identifying with the dominant ideology and yet are expected to act on its premises. In their role as cultural brokers, the workers try vainly to interpret and apply the law in a culturally sensitive manner.

The Inuit workers' attempts to define their mandate in practice is hampered by their isolation and the highly individualized nature of their work. While their geographic and administrative distance from the bureaucracy may appear advantageous to developing an alternative approach to the work, it in fact deprives workers of a supportive network within which to develop appropriate norms of practice.

I will now consider the local context of the workers' practice, examining how this setting exacerbates the difficulties workers experience as they attempt to define and implement the youth protection mandate.

YOUTH PROTECTION IN A COMMUNITY CONTEXT

The Village as Practice Setting

Statutory practice generates anxiety associated with the exercise of authority and discretion, particularly in the high-risk area of child abuse. Making decisions about the welfare of children is all the more problematic for Inuit workers because of the intimacy of their relationship to the community. The majority of workers are practicing in small villages where they have close family ties.

The possibility of having to intervene in their own extended families causes workers a great deal of discomfort. One woman described her situation this way.

> Sometimes I think it is an advantage for me to be in a small community. I know everyone pretty well and if there is a problem, I usually hear about it very soon. But many of the people in this village are relatives of mine. It is very hard for me to think about going into their homes and telling them that they are not good parents. To investigate my own family would cause me, and them, a lot of pain. I would not want to cause people in my family to take sides against me or against each other.

The fear of disrupting family ties and provoking divided loyalties is distressing for this worker and suggests to her a need for extraordinary caution. When workers must intervene in their extended families, objectivity is regarded as pretentious; as a result, they risk being criticized for engaging in preferential treatment.

As observed by the worker quoted above, the small size of northern communities can be an advantage for workers insofar as their familiarity with the residents may permit them to better anticipate problems and to intervene early. However, the small size of the communities often precludes confidentiality and invites an intense degree of public scrutiny of a worker's performance.

A worker can be readily observed going to and from clients' homes; her interactions with other professionals in the village elicits their interest in the outcomes of her work; the cases on which she is working are sometimes made public when a parent or family member shares their experience with social services on the local FM radio; and cases typically involve a large cast of players including an extensive family network both within and beyond the village. In addition, workers feel considerable pressure to lead exemplary lives lest they be taken for hypocrites. A number of female workers, in particular, noted the additional pressure they feel to be good mothers and wives in the face of their responsibility to assess the adequacy of others' parenting and household management.

The social organization of northern communities is especially significant for workers because it precludes the separation of public and private life enjoyed by social workers in the south. Without this distinction, it is impossible to achieve the social distance from clients that normally helps to protect workers from the emotional impact of their day-to-day work.[16]

Thus, Inuit workers are unusually vulnerable to repercussions from their decisions and are quick to personalize criticisms of their practice. Given their cultural and family ties to the community, Inuit workers are likely to identify with and be influenced by their clients' perspectives and, therefore, to experience extreme tension in the exercise of authority and discretion. This tension is particularly acute when agency and community expectations of worker practice are incompatible with one another.

Conflicting Expectations: Community Versus Agency

The geographic and structural location of community workers heightens the divergence in service orientation that characterizes any core-periphery arrangement of services. Johnson found that an orientation to client rather than administrative needs is more likely to characterise the work of practitioners close to the periphery whose relationships with clients are more meaningful and immediate than those with socially distant colleagues and superiors.[17] This is certainly the case of Inuit workers. Given the local situation described above, it is not surprising that Inuit workers feel a need to be especially mindful of community perceptions of their practice.

At the same time, however, community workers are accountable to the agency for their interventions and so cannot afford to lose sight of administrative expectations of their work (i.e., statistical reports, properly maintained files, well-documented case interventions). Although the agency's monitoring of worker performance is far less intense than that which they experience from local residents, the pressure for workers to comply with bureaucratic expectations is considerable nonetheless. Youth protection is acknowledged by administrators and workers alike to be a high-risk area of social work practice. The risk of being held responsible in the event of a tragedy (i.e., death of a child) is that much greater for a worker who has not complied with agency standards.

Problems arise, however, when the activity required to satisfy agency demands is deemed unacceptable by one or another source in the village. All of the workers have had some experience of this conflict. Reflecting on her experience with a case of alleged sexual abuse, a worker recalled that:

> After I interviewed the child to get her story, and she was upset and crying, the mother did not want me to talk to her daughter again. She was worried that this would upset her more. And one of the teachers too said that maybe I should leave the child alone, that she would tell somebody when she was ready. People were getting angry with me for going around and asking lots of questions.

In this particular case, the worker went on to explain that even though several weeks had elapsed since her initial interventions, she continued to feel that she should resume the investigation. The worker was upset about not having done a thorough job although she had taken measures to protect the child from the alleged perpetrator.

In addition to the personal discomfort and anxiety which youth protection workers may experience in dealing with cases of child sexual abuse, this worker was also confronted with the strong cultural sanction against interference in people's personal lives.

While it is impossible to assess the relative weight of these factors on the worker's decision, we can see that, when taken together, these conditions might easily deter even the most conscientious worker from attempting anything more than an expeditious solution (i.e., removal of the child). In this example, the need to attend to both agency demands for a thorough investigation and community norms of personal autonomy left the worker feeling caught, and ultimately, distressed about not having done a good job. The conflicting norms of conduct that community workers encounter in such cases make it very difficult for them to decide whose expectations should be given precedence, those of the agency or those of the community. The need to remain sensitive to both compounds the difficulty that workers encounter in trying to define appropriate norms of practice. As a result, day-to-day practice varies considerably from one community to the next and tends to be only vaguely defined in each village.

The Problem of Diffuse Role Boundaries

The community workers report that they do not know the legislation and structure of social services well enough to be able to clearly articulate the nature and limits of their various roles (youth protection worker, worker for young offenders, home care coordinator) to village residents. Their inability to do so, coupled with the lack of public awareness of social services, generates considerable confusion for both workers and clients.

As might be expected under these circumstances, workers often receive requests for service which fall beyond the scope of their various mandated responsibilities. Yet, turning people away is difficult. As "the only show in town," workers face the additional burden of not being able to refer applicants to an alternative resource. Nor do they want to risk being judged as uncaring or dismissive. For example, the Inuit workers are frequently called upon by other professionals (medical, judicial) and community residents to act as interpreters, which is an accepted part of the more traditional helper role. An experienced female worker explained:

> These cases take a lot of my time because, most of the time, that person needs to fill out papers so I end up writing for them. I spent a lot of time last week helping a woman write a declaration for the police so they could lay charges against her husband. It took a long time to explain to her why they needed the information and to help her put together the details of her story. But I felt that I had to help her because I know something about these things and she really didn't know what to do. These kinds of situations bring me lots of extra work because I sometimes then have to spend time counselling the person, listening to their troubles and supporting them.

While the extra demands on her time may be considerable, requests for assistance of this kind have a compelling quality about them; not only is the worker able to easily avert any untoward criticism for lack of responsiveness, but she is also able to provide a concrete service to the client, thereby increasing the likelihood that her intervention will be genuinely helpful and thus, personally gratifying.

The provision of concrete services, which figured prominently in traditional helping, is highly regarded and frequently expected by community residents. By contrast, the more abstract services typical of the professional social work role, (i.e., counselling) are less likely to be gratifying for clients or workers. In light of this, it is easy to appreciate why community workers may continue to identify the more traditional aspects of their helping role as appropriate responsibilities in their current practice. Yet, by responding to requests for service that fall beyond the scope of their mandates, workers inadvertently perpetuate the confusion surrounding their role. Further, the wide range of activities and additional demands on worker time promote a sense of crisis-orientation in their practice and leaves workers feeling that they have no control over their work.

For social workers in public agencies, this problem is generally resolved to some extent by their colleagues and supervisory staff. This primary reference group not only provides workers with much needed support, but also serves as a structure within which to develop guides for day-to-day practice activity. Through association with colleagues, workers generate what Rees terms "practice oriented ideologies"and a consensus around appropriate norms of practice that help them to make sense of the demands of their job (i.e., caseload size, resource limitations). For example, a casework ideology would lead workers to give precedence to situations appearing to require ongoing intervention of a therapeutic nature. Rees maintains that the importance of practice oriented ideologies is twofold: they enable workers to perceive appropriate roles for themselves, and they give workers some sense of control in a job which confronts them with a range of baffling problems (Rees 1978: 52-60).

The Inuit workers, however, are geographically so far removed from their front-line colleagues and administrative personnel that it is virtually impossible to align themselves with either group as a point of reference for clarifying day-to-day practice. Although the community workers may want some guidance and direction from village members, the lack of consensus at the local level constrains the latter group's capacity and willingness to assist workers in this area. Consequently, the community workers find themselves struggling independently to make sense of the demands of the job. This particular condition of the work not only contributes to a highly idiosyncratic approach to practice, but also to intense feelings of alienation among the workers. Regrettably, no concrete steps are being taken at either the community or organizational level to deal with these outcomes.

The foregoing analysis suggests that the community worker is perceived by members of the village as a 'person' with traditional (ascribed) status of one sort or another (woman, mother, elder, etc.) deriving from a matrix of her characteristics. On the other hand, she is seen by her agency as a 'worker' with activities deriving from that role exclusively. The village personalizes her and the agency objectifies her. Also, the wide mandate for various kinds of interventions probably fits better with a village idea of a generalist, personalized helper than would a highly specialized role.

The problem in part seems to be that the helping role is by definition monopolized through access to resources, thus devaluing other sorts of aid by others. For the worker, the problem for the worker includes lack of guidance with respect to triage (which mandate takes precedence?) and in a lack of resources (triage decisions become impossibly difficult under pressures of extreme scarcity).

Isolation and Lack of Support

Social workers need to be supported in their work as they are continually faced with anxiety-provoking and often intractable situations that as a profession they claim to be able to do something about (Spencer 1973: 4-7). In youth protection work, particularly in the area of child abuse, workers need support and protection to negotiate the risk associated with the exercise of discretion and their own power. They also need the opportunity to talk over candidly what they think and feel and their doubts about their work. The risk for social workers is that they themselves may interpret such doubts as indicative of personal inadequacy, a judgement which undermines their self-confidence and sense of competence to do the job.

At present, there is no effective structure in place to adequately support Inuit workers in their day-to-day work. Inuit workers often experience their communities as unsupportive environments in which to practice.

This worker's observations about her own community reflects their shared experience.

> People do not understand what it is that we have to do. They don't know how difficult it is to do this work. And many of them think that it is just 'our' job, that it's up to us, because we are the community workers, to solve all of the problems in the community. But the problems are too big; we cannot do it alone.

The residents' lack of support and understanding, in conjunction with their uncertainty about the law, has resulted in considerable suspicion regarding worker motives, and in some cases, where the outcome of worker interventions have been judged unfavourable, a lack of trust and even outright hostility toward the worker. Fear for their safety is a common experience, particularly among female workers. Other professionals in the village who might usually be regarded as potential sources of support often are not perceived this way by the workers. Many of the workers report serious problems in communication with other service providers, and with few exceptions, they have been unsuccessful in establishing good collaborative working relationships with them. Although a supervising social worker used to make regular visits to workers in their villages, these visits have been largely curtailed. The lack of organizational support is felt keenly by workers. For example, this experienced worker's sense of abandonment is very clear.

> It's been a very long time since a social worker came to this community. The social worker used to come and talk with the workers about their cases and give us support. We could see that they know how difficult it is to do the work here, and it was good to be able to talk with the supervisor. But now they never come; nobody even comes here. That's why now the community workers feel we are on our own.

At present, workers can expect to meet with a supervisor at the outset of their employment. During these contacts the emphasis is placed on familiarizing the new worker with administrative requirements and procedures (i.e., case registration, statistical reports, setting up client files). While the community workers allow that these are important components of their preparation, supervision of this kind clearly is intended to be time-limited and does not speak to the workers' ongoing needs for learning and support.

Once a worker has been fully oriented to the system's needs, she is left on her own with the option to call the supervisor or Director of Youth Protection (DYP) for consultation and direction on specific case-related difficulties. While community workers appreciate being able to contact these individuals to ask for direction, especially at the outset of an investigation, there are inherent limitations of such supervision. As suggested by this worker's account of her interaction with head office:

> Most of the time when I call the supervisor or DYP it's because I have a new case and I have to let them know that. Sometimes when I am stuck with a problem on a case I will call to ask what they think I should do. Or I call one of the workers in another village, especially if I know they have good experience with some kinds of problems. But we don't talk like this, like we have been doing this past week. We don't ever talk about the things that bother us, except maybe we complain about forms and paperwork, little things like that.

While the emphasis on procedural matters is to some extent supportive of workers because it helps them to structure their interventions and offers some measure of protection around the decisions they must take, this focus discourages any discussion of the workers' feelings about their practice and leaves them to struggle alone with their doubts and fears. Ultimately, the community workers are left feeling vulnerable and exposed and unable to rely on either the agency or community.

Climate of Despondency About Community Worker Practice

Like all social workers, the community workers feel that their interventions should improve their clients' lives. Yet in reality, workers' efforts often are of limited benefit, and in some instances, possibly even detrimental to clients.[18] The limited effectiveness of worker interventions is in part a direct consequence of inadequate resources with which to do the work. The problem of limited resources affects the practice of all social workers in state agencies and constrains their ability to respond to clients in a fully human way, contributing to feelings of frustration and powerlessness. However, the situation confronting Inuit workers is unusually drastic: there are few substitute care resources; there are long delays between court dates; there are no treatment resources for substance abusers, and so on. Recounting her experience in the case of a sexually abused child whose father was awaiting prosecution, one worker reported that:

> There was going to be a long wait for the court to come and the police did not remove the father from the community. So it was impossible to keep the child here. She had to go to a foster home in another community until there was court. This was very hard for the girl, the mother, and the brothers and sisters, too. The child ends up being punished while the father gets to stay with his family. I know that already the child was feeling bad because all her family was upset. When she had to go away, I'm sure she must have felt even worse. But all of us felt, the child, the mother and me, that there was no other way to protect her from the father.

The worker's responsibility to protect the child in this case required that she resign herself to placing the child outside her own community—an unsatisfactory arrangement considering the child's emotional needs. In cases like this, workers cannot help but question the value of their interventions.

The lack of appropriate resources to offer clients, in conjunction with the material impoverishment of their clients' lives, leaves workers feeling helpless. The Inuit workers recognize all too well the limitations of what they can do for clients. Sharing her frustration about the work, one woman observed that:

> I feel useless in many cases because I can't give clients what they need to solve their problem. If a battered woman wants to get away from her husband and take her children, the best thing is for her to have another house, maybe here or in another village. But there are no extra houses. She would have to wait for a long time. And for her to go to another community means that she will lose her friends and the support of her family.

Another worker echoed these sentiments when she reported that:

> Sometimes I think that the help I give people is no good, it doesn't change very much. A mother who asked for help with her daughter, she was fifteen and using drugs, told me after a long time that she should never have brought her daughter to social services because now she is worse, her behaviour has gotten worse. With another case like this one, I don't know what I would do. I feel powerless with some of the problems.

The workers' sense of helplessness in such cases is enhanced by the extent of certain social problems in their communities (i.e., substance abuse and violence). Workers feel, and rightly so, that while their interventions might make a difference in the short run, in the final analysis their efforts do little to change things. In light of this, it is difficult for community workers to go on justifying and defending their interventions to the community and to themselves. The apparent futility of their efforts generates a pervasive sense of despondency.

Socialization to the Profession

Thus far, we have seen how the various contexts of the Inuit workers' practice construct a very particular experience of youth protection work. I have noted in particular how the workers' day-to-day practice is fraught with conflict, much of which arises from the imposition of the State's definition and organization of statutory work, and a simultaneous lack of resources. While it is clear that all social workers within state bureaucracy feel constrained by the organizational and social context of youth protection work, practitioners in the south are better able to resist excessive bureaucratic control of practice. Their ability to do so derives from their identification with the professional model of social work practice.

I turn now to consider the Inuit community workers' socialization to the profession to examine how this process sustains rather than mitigates the conflicts and tensions that they experience.

From Lay Helper to Professional Social Worker

Socialization to the profession of social work involves relinquishing lay conceptions of what helping is about. As we have seen, this is difficult for Inuit community workers, in part because their lay conception of helping is informed by a cultural tradition that embodies values and norms of conduct that have little place within contemporary views of professional helping.

Inuit are socialized to a tradition of undifferentiated helping, whereas professional helping is grounded in a functional division of labour. In the functionalist tradition of social work, the worker's professional identity derives from the specific activities of the agency rather than from a generalist commitment.

The residual influence of Inuit tradition is manifested in current hiring practices. The community, through its leaders, recommends certain of its members to the social service agency as appropriate candidates for employment as community workers. Suitability for the work is judged by the community on the basis of personal qualities deemed essential in a good social worker: the potential worker must inspire trust in others, be someone to whom others feel they can turn for advice and support, and must have the respect of others.

While the agency appreciates the desirability of these qualities, it is particularly interested in hiring individuals who demonstrate sufficient proficiency in English to be able to acquire the knowledge and skills essential to meeting organizational needs (i.e., for written reports for accountability and court purposes). Ironically, all official documents are in French which none of the workers read.[19]

The agency's preference not only limits the pool of potential workers, but also results in the hiring of younger people less likely to satisfy community criteria. Those hired without the approbation of their community have a very difficult time establishing credibility. An experienced older worker observed that:

> The young workers have a really hard time because the community does not show much respect for their opinion and judgement. And the community will not support someone that they don't respect. Of course, this makes the work even harder.

State control of hiring undermines the social bases of recruitment, thereby depriving community workers of the forms of sponsorship and potential sources of legitimation crucial to successful practice at the local level (Johnson 1973: 79). Thus, the discrepancy between lay and professional conceptions of a suitable candidate is resolved at the expense of individual workers. There are few individuals in the north who satisfy both agency and community criteria for employment, and even those who do cannot help but feel that, ultimately, they will never quite measure up to agency standards of professional practice.

Professionalization of Inuit Workers

The feelings of inadequacy which community workers expressed arise in part from their inability to conduct their youth protection practice in the prescribed way. As we have seen, the bureaucratic norms of public administration do not fit the practice reality in the north; attempts to make them do so are bound to generate frustration. At the same time, however, Inuit workers are socialized to a professional model of social work practice that claims expert knowledge as a legitimating principle.

The process of what Pearson terms "joining the club" typically begins for students in universities or colleges where liberal professional ideologies of social work practice remain dominant.[20] Much emphasis is placed on the training and competence of individual caseworkers. The therapeutic casework relationship continues to be at the core of what is deemed professional social work, and it remains the basis for claims to specialized knowledge and status. In addition, professional ideologies posit social workers as autonomous, competent, professional experts.[21]

Identification with the professional social work culture is an important aspect of formal training as it provides workers with a self-protective armour. As Pearson notes,

> professional culture has the important function of offering ready-made, routinized 'solutions' as opposed to solutions which are grounded in the complex moral calculus of welfare services.[22]

Without the armour of routine professionalism, workers would be repeatedly confronted by the moral and political dilemmas which lie behind their practice decisions. At the same time, the internalization of professional ideologies of practice enables social workers to better resist excessive bureaucratic control of their work. In this regard, the community workers find themselves at a real disadvantage.

The vast majority of community workers are trained subsequent to their hiring. As students registered in the McGill University Certificate Program in Northern Social Work Practice, the community workers participate in a series of two-week long, intensive training sessions offered in the north by full-time faculty and sessional lectures from the McGill School of Social Work. The emphasis in these credit courses to date has been placed on issues that the community workers themselves have identified as crucial to their learning, and on orientation to the relevant legislation and the Québec social service structure.

At some point during their employment, workers can expect to have a two week period of closely supervised practice during which the integration of social work theory and practice is emphasized.[23] Just recently, experienced community workers have started to take an active role in the course preparation and teaching. Their participation helps to ensure the relevance of course content and sensitivity to cultural differences, as well as allowing much of the teaching to be offered in Inuktitut.

Within the social service organization itself, hierarchical supervision on case-related issues provides additional opportunities for training; however, the emphasis here is placed on teaching workers the bureaucratic and administrative requirements of the job. Given the sporadic nature of both the training sessions and direct supervision of worker practice, Inuit workers have little opportunity to consolidate new learning in such a way that it enhances their sense of confidence and competence to do the work.

The community workers' weak professionalization has two outstanding consequences. First, the Inuit workers lack professional confidence and a sense of professional identity. As a result, it is difficult for them to resist the administrative, bureaucratic apparatus in the same way that southern workers might. In order to do so, the community workers would need to perceive themselves as the competent experts that professional ideology teaches social workers that they are. The community workers, however, do not consider themselves to be professional experts, nor are they accorded this status by the agency, as suggested by this worker's observations.

> It's really not fair that we are called 'community workers' and that we don't get paid as much as social workers. Even if we don't have a degree, there are other things we have, like knowledge of our people and the community. A person needs this to work in the north. And besides that, the bosses expect us to do the same job as a social worker. It is very hard to get our people to understand what we do. A community worker could be someone who drives the water truck or picks up the garbage. You know, those people get paid more than we do!

This worker's frustration and sense of being devalued by the agency was shared by all of the community workers interviewed. The knowledge that the Inuit workers bring to the job is not valued by the agency except to the extent that it enables them to satisfy organizational needs (i.e., workers' ability to speak Inuktitut facilitates service delivery). Although the workers are deemed by the agency to be less qualified to do the work than accredited social workers, and are remunerated accordingly, they are nevertheless expected to perform the same tasks. Thus, community workers conclude that the agency regards their work as inferior, and it is difficult for them to feel competent in their dealings with clients or the bureaucracy.

A second critical outcome of the Inuit workers' socialization to the profession is that they find themselves without a reference group in their day-to-day practice. As noted earlier, this deprives workers of a supportive environment in which to define appropriate norms of conduct in their youth protection practice. Moreover, it means that no one is assisting the community workers with what Berger terms the "ideological work" that is required to legitimate their role at the organizational and community level.[24] As a result, Inuit workers continue to experience a stark disjunction between divergent conceptions of their role and practice, and they remain unable to sanction their own use of authority.[25]

In the current context of the Inuit workers' youth protection practice, both professional ideology and bureaucratic norms of public administration function to perpetuate the community workers' feelings of inadequacy and subordination. Moreover, the sources of legitimation available to community workers within the contemporary definitions of statutory practice appear to be incompatible with potential sources at the community level. How are the community workers attempting to address their need for legitimation and support at the local level, and what do their efforts tell us about the ongoing conceptual and practical development of an indigenous approach to youth protection?

Redefining Youth Protection Practice

The notion of professional autonomy is problematic for all front-line workers in youth protection services. While the ideology of professional autonomy implies that social workers should be capable of functioning independently in a sure and competent manner, the reality is that workers seldom feel this way when confronted with the risks and uncertainty of decision-making around the welfare of children (Davies 1985).

The discomfort associated with the exercise of authority and discretion is exacerbated for community workers by their lack of professional identity and legitimation. Given the current organizational and social context of statutory practice, it is clear that in order to reduce these tensions, Inuit workers need to look to the community for alternative sources of legitimation and support in their work.

In some of the villages, workers can seek support from the local social advisory committee. However, these do not exist in all communities, and where they have participated in case discussion and planning with the workers, the outcomes have not always been very satisfactory from the workers' point of view. They cite a number of reasons for this: the workers and committee members are not clear about their respective mandates and what they can expect from each other; the advice of the committee may not fit with the worker's own opinion of the best way to proceed on a case; and members sometimes resent being asked to volunteer their time to assist a worker who is, after all, being paid to deal with the problem at hand.

In those instances where workers have found the committee's participation to be helpful, this has been largely as a result of the legitimating function that the committee provides for the worker. Recounting her experience of requesting the committee's support in order to gain access to a family in which the mother was being beaten by her husband, one worker observed that she felt more secure and confident presenting her concerns to the couple in the presence of the advisory committee. The sense of security afforded the worker and the permission to intervene that she derives from meetings with the committee and client are important factors in her decision to become actively involved with the family. The sanction provided by the committee serves to alter the clients' perception of the worker's role. Her intervention comes to be seen as less intrusive or coercive than potential alternatives such as police and court involvement. At the same time, the committee's participation serves to diminish the worker's sense of individual responsibility for the case. It may be, as well, that meetings such as these are particularly helpful to the worker because they replicate the more traditional approach to intervention into family matters which relied upon a process of consensual decision-making to arrive at a plan of action.

The foregoing example of community participation in the worker's youth protection practice contains a number of important lessons concerning the future direction of statutory work in the north. Below, I will summarize these lessons and suggest how they can further the conceptual and practical development of an indigenous approach to youth protection.

Conclusions

The initiative taken by Inuit workers to actively engage the community in their practice is a creative response to the demands of the job at the local level. The benefit of such a strategy for community workers is considerable. By involving the advisory committee, workers may obtain a clear sanction for their work and thus, the legitimation that is crucial to their exercise of authority. The committee's participation serves to diminish the extreme isolation that community workers experience and permits a shared responsibility for decision making and case planning. In addition, the intervention strategies that emerge from this process better reflect the traditional approach to problem solving and the norms and realities of Inuit village life.

The limited success of committee participation to date reflects the continued dominance of the State's definition and organization of statutory practice. However, it also speaks to the current lack of consensus at the local level concerning the role of youth protection services more generally. Such a consensus will be difficult to achieve given the legacy of divisiveness within communities that has come about in part as a consequence of thirty years of white tutelage. Yet, by virtue of the success that has been achieved in individual cases, there is reason to be optimistic that ultimately practice norms will be defined through worker collaboration with the social and political structures already in place at the local level.

While community support is crucial to the ongoing development of an indigenous approach to youth protection, this objective requires more than active community participation to be realized. In addition, the workers need the support of a reference group in which to validate their practice experiences with one another and to achieve a clear definition of their identity as community workers. By engaging in a self-reflective analysis of their own practice, Inuit workers may begin to develop practice guidelines that better reflect the realities of the north. Thereby, they may achieve a beginning sense of control over their work. However, these initiatives cannot be undertaken without organizational support.

Clearly the issue of control is central to future developments in the area of youth protection services in the north. The empirical evidence suggests that the form and content of statutory work imposed by the State simply do not fit the norms and realities of Inuit village life. The experience of Inuit workers demonstrates that the hierarchical relations of control engendered by the bureaucratic organization of youth protection work are untenable at the local level. In order to achieve even minimal resolution of the fundamental conflicts in their day-to-day practice, Inuit workers must share their power and decision-making authority with the community.

The organizational commitment to facilitating this process has yet to move beyond the level of rhetoric. To actively support the workers' efforts in this regard would imply facilitating, albeit indirectly, the development of a local constituency which could eventually threaten state control of services. It remains to be seen whether the Québec State is prepared to question the correctness of its views.

NOTES

1. See Chapter 15 of the Agreement, "Health and Social Services (Inuit)", Articles 15.0.21, 15.0.24 and 15.0.26.
2. Lesemann examines how the ideals envisioned in the Castonguay recommendations for comprehensive, accessible, community based services were compromised by the bureaucratization of social services.
3. For a discussion of the ideological shift in child welfare, see Nigel Parton, "Child Abuse, Social Anxiety and Welfare", *British Journal of Social Work* (1981): 11, 319-414. Parton's analysis, however, tends to be overly deterministic in that he fails to take into account the contradictions inherent in statutory work, for example, between the care and control elements in practice. For an analysis of the contradictory nature of child welfare policy and practice, see Steve Bolger, Paul Corrigan, Jan Docking and Nick Frost, *Towards Socialist Welfare Work* (London: MacMillan, 1981: 82-107).
4. Originated by Stanley Cohen, the term "moral panic" describes a situation in which the societal reaction to a perceived threat is out of all proportion to its empirical reality. See Stanley Cohen, *Folk Devils and Moral Panics* (Hammondsworth: Penguin, 1971). Parton examines the role of moral panic as a mechanism of ideological shift in statutory child welfare. See Parton, 319-414.
5. Since 1985 in Québec, extensive media coverage has been focused on child abuse cases allegedly demonstrating "how the system failed" (*Montréal Gazette* December 14, 1985); "how agency ignored kids' plight"

(*Montréal Gazette* February 4, 1987); or worse, how child protection services are in "a shambles" (*Montréal Gazette* January 24, 1987).
6. Institutionalized racism consists of the laws and relationships built into major social institutions that act to promote existing inequality and the social exclusion of minority groups. See Brad McKenzie, "Social Work Practice with Native People", in Shankar A. Yelaga, ed., *An Introduction to Social Work Practice in Canada*, (Scarborough: Prentice Hall, 1985: 272-288).
7. See any of the following for an analysis of this process: Hugh Brody, *The People's Land: Eskimos and Whites in the Eastern Arctic*, (Aylesbury: Penguin Books, 1975); Robert Paine, "The Nursery Game"; Evelyn Kallen, *Ethnicity and Human Rights in Canada* (Toronto: Gage Publishing, 1983); James Frideres, *Native People in Canada: Contemporary Conflicts* (Scarborough: Prentice Hall, 1983); B. Singh Bolaria and Peter S. Li, *Racial Oppression in Canada* (Toronto: Garamond Press, 1985).
8. Kallen describes the paternalistic model as highly asymmetric with vast disparities in political, economic and social power between the dominant and subordinate groups. The more powerful, dominant population is highly ethnocentric, and it is the normative imperatives of the dominant ethnic group which become sanctioned in law and incorporated into public institutional policies thereby providing the moral and cultural guidelines for the whole society. Evelyn Kallen, *Ethnicity and Human Rights In Canada* (1983).
9. Paine notes that tutelage is based upon conformity whose inducements include subtle coercions and implies a relationship in which manifest superiority is attributed to the tutor, in this case, white administrators. Paine, "The Nursey Game": 8.
10. *Ibid.*, 20. In conjunction with personal autonomy and flexibility, deference in one's behaviour towards others is highly valued in Inuit society. Deference includes people being patient with one another, not pressing one another to conform, not trying to change or reform each other, and withdrawing from strong, threatening interpersonal relations.
11. Jean Briggs, "Strategies of perception: the management of ethnic identity" in Robert Paine, ed., *Patrons and Brokers in the East Arctic* (St. John's: Memorial University, 1971: 55-72).
12. Geoffrey Pearson, "The politics of uncertainty: a study in the socialization of the social worker" in Howard Jones, ed., *Towards a New Social Work* (London: Routledge & Kegan Paul, 1975: 48).
13. Davies notes that there is not a direct unilinear relationship between a set of rules and practitioners' adherence to them, that workers intervene in this relationship through their exercise of discretion. Moreover, she argues that one possible consequence of social workers' need for protection and the bureaucratic nature of management's response may be a shift from a therapeutic to a bureaucratic, procedural consciousness. See Davies, chapter 6.
14. For an analysis of the contradictory nature of statutory practice and the implications for front-line workers, see Bolger *et al.*, "Child care decisions", 82-107. See also Carole Satyamurti, "Care and control in local authority social work" in Noel Parry, Michael Rustin and Carole Satyamurti, eds., *Social Work, Welfare and the State* (London: Edward Arnold, 1979: 89-103); Davies, chapter 5.

15. Roles associated with the regulatory functions of child welfare are of particular concern to Native people because they tend to perpetuate the historical patterns of dependency created by the colonization process unless they are exercised in ways which recognize both cultural sensitivity and the political aspirations of Native people. Brad McKenzie, 272-288. See also Peter Hudson and Brad Mckenzie, "Child welfare and Native people: the extension of colonialism", *The Social Worker* 1981: 49; 63-66, 87-89.
16. Satyamurti found that although in principle social workers disliked the aloofness implied in the idea of a professional relationship, in practice they felt that they had to maintain some social distance between themselves and their clients, as otherwise it would be more difficult to exercise authority if the necessity arose. Somtimes what they had in mind was an eventuality involving direct coercion (i.e., removal of a child). See Satyamurti, 96-97.
17. Johnson examines how the localism of practice is in part a consequence of state mediation of social services. See Terence Johnson, *Professions and Power* (London: MacMillan, 1973: 81).
18. Rees found that it was common for social workers to sometimes doubt the usefulness of their job and not see it as likely to affect change in individual cases let alone on wider social and political fronts. See Stuart Rees, 48.
19. Community workers would prefer that all written documentation, (i.e., court orders, agreements for service) be available in Inuktitut to ensure their clients' understanding of the material.
20. Pearson notes how, compared with the lavish care spent on helping students to develop casework and relationship skills, there is minimal effort to help them relate to the complex personal, moral and political force fields of social welfare. See Geoffrey Pearson, "Making social workers: bad promises and good omens" in Roy Bailey and Mike Brake, *eds.*, *Radical Social Work* (London: Edward Arnold, 1975: 38).
21. Lionel Groulx, "Les critiques du modele professionel en service sociale: enjeux ideologiques et politiques."
22. Pearson, Politics of uncertainity, 48.
23. Written proposals for the training of community workers, prepared by Professor Liesel Urtnowski at McGill, in addition to fieldnotes from her teaching experience on the Hudson and Ungava Bay coasts, provided an important source of documentary evidence in this research project.
24. Berger describes remedial ideological work as an interpretive process which constructs a set of legitimations or arguments aimed at coping with dissonances. See Bennett Berger, *The Survival of a Counterculture: Ideological Work and Everyday Life Among Communards* (Berkeley: University of California Press, 1981: 89).
25. To sanction one's own use of authority, an individual must be clear about what is required of her, competent to undertake the task, and able to manage the ambivalence implicit in the exercise of such authority. See Herschel Prins, "Authority and the Casework Relationship", *Social Work* (1962: 19; 21).

Chapter Five

COMMUNITY BASED PRACTICE: POLITICAL ALTERNATIVES OR NEW STATE FORMS?

Eric Shragge

The founding and the development of community-based alternative organizations in Montréal from the 1960s to the present has raised both hopeful possibilities for, and illusions of, social change. These efforts, whether providing social and health services or promoting economic development often based on a progressive social vision and a model of 'community empowerment', have had contradictory results. At times, in their form of organization, ideologies, and content of their activities these organizations have acted as radical alternatives. They have been part of wider challenges to the social institutions of patriarchal capitalism. On the other hand, despite their origins in radical social movements, many of these organizations have been drawn into, or have become extensions of, state programs providing social and health services or support systems for private economic development. Most fall between these two poles. The goal of this essay is to explore these contradictions and tensions in two types of organizations: Alternative Service Organizations (ASOs) and organizations involved in Community Economic Development (CED).

The current context provides community activists with tough choices. The government, through a variety of programs, have offered support to community organizations, but the trade-off is that groups may have to sacrifice their autonomy that had, in the past, led to independent action. There is a danger that this process will draw the groups into a partnership with the State, and completely neutralize them as an effective oppositional voice. A recent government paper on its orientation to the social and health services develops this position with clarity. It states:

> The community organizations acquire the status of partners associated in the pursuit of a common objective: improvement of the public's health and well-being...the two levels are working together (Gouvernement du Québec 1989: 78).

In itself, a common objective is not explicitly threatening to the autonomy of community groups but in the context of changes in the community and social change movements in Québec, the problem becomes more serious. Fauvreau (1989) states that beginning in the 1980s there has been a relative demobilization of popular and community groups, a crisis in leadership which weakens them, in their perspectives, and in their internal functioning. Panet-Raymond (1989) asks whether or not groups can maintain their autonomy, given the pressures put on them by the State in the context of the redefinition of the welfare State, such as shifting state services to the community through the use of volunteers, community organizations and the family. Funds from the State become available for specific functions, thus limiting groups in the establishment of their own agendas and practices.

Practitioners of community development and organization can see these developments as representing yet another challenge. The power of the State to define and shape practice through the control of funding, is always present, but groups have, in many ways, resisted the pressures of this control, and found ways to develop and maintain their autonomy. With autonomy, these groups have acted in opposition to state policy, or mobilized and organized individuals to empower themselves confronting the forces of capitalism and patriarchy that shape their everyday life. The ability of these types of organizations to develop autonomy and independent community practice that is oppositional in its form of organization and program content, will also be examined.

Can these community organizations through the provision of a service or through their involvement in CED act, at the same time, as a means of challenging the patterns of social and economic domination? In other words, despite the tendency in the literature to separate community action from community development (in this instance as service delivery) (Carniol 1985), this essay will examine approaches to community practice that bring together a form of community provision that, at least in its origins, aimed to provide a community service and, at the same time, challenge, in a radical way, the dominant order. The underlying, and longer-term question is, can these forms of practice remain intact over time *without*—as a result of political 'purity'—moving to the margins of community life or becoming 'coopted' by state funding, which as a consequence, eliminates their change-oriented component? This balance between service and community change is central. As well, the issue of the alternative ways of providing a service gives these organizations a change-oriented image, and is a major way of linking the service-orientation with demands for social change.

What Makes an Organization an Alternative?

Before turning to the discussion of the particular example of community intervention, a brief definition of the meaning of alternatives will be presented.

There is no simple definition for what constitutes an alternative, and even if one were possible, no organization would fit into it exactly. Rather than a utopian preconception of the ideal organization, existing approaches used by organizations will be emphasized. Features or aspects of alternatives will be presented so that we can see that parts of groups and organizations do, in fact, embody some of these characteristics. The concepts developed here will be applied in discussions of both ASOs and CED.

The first characteristic is that of program content or the activities of the organizations. There is a tendency in organizations funded by the State or private federations (i.e., Centraide, United Way) to substitute service delivery for political action. For example, in housing, groups providing information on rights, on an individual basis, have been given greater access to funds than those groups organizing tenants. Work at the individual level becomes a priority over attempts to organize and to mobilize victims of social injustice. The content of program becomes defined as individual service rather than collective action. For an organization to remain an alternative it would have to link the political with the personal. This does not imply that individual services are not provided, but rather service to the individual is linked to political and/or social change. Thus, the program must have at least some political content, linked to individual service, in order to be considered alternative.

Next, the form of organization should be as non-hierarchical as possible in order to provide the opportunity for staff or community participation in a significant way (i.e., more than token representation of staff and community as client representatives). A democratic structure and process of decision-making should be present. There are many options that organizations have used including direct elections to boards from open community assemblies, worker collectives, structures that guarantee representation from community organizations, and structures that allow various forms of representation of workers, community and clients. In contrast to state organizations, which allow token representation at best, and in which power is highly centralized, alternatives can be characterized by their attempts to share power and decision making between workers, community representatives, and clients of the agency.

Another characteristic of alternatives—whether they be services or community economic development—is the emphasis, particularly in their origins, on the hiring and training of community residents rather than employing university or college-trained professionals. This emphasis is a reflection of attempts to de-mystify the knowledge of professionals, and help empower community residents. There are many tensions and contradictions in this position, particularly because in many instances, 'radical' professionals initiated and supported these projects. As well, the employment of non-professionals leads to low paying and insecure jobs in these agencies and, subsequently, these alternative groups become low cost options to state services.

An alternative approach can include an emphasis on social change, as well as a service orientation, a structure that features democratic forms of participation of worker, community, and clients, and an emphasis on the use of non-professionals. These characteristics, usually stronger in the beginning phases of the alternative organization, remain as its development unfolds. We will see however, that these traditions are difficult to maintain in the face of pressures resulting from external, usually government funding. Yet, these characteristics may not be eliminated entirely, and their existence emphasizes the complex relationship between State and community alternatives.

How have these alternative services and community economic development organizations fared in relation to the issues discussed above? Do they constitute a form of community practice that addresses the short-coming of the community action and development approaches presented earlier? Can they become at least part of, or the seeds of, a democratic option to the welfare State? Do they embody characteristics that would allow their classification as alternative to the State and more 'traditional' agencies, for example, based on their structures (democratic vs. hierarchical), their content or activities (only individual service vs. linking service and political/social change) and/or their hiring practice (professionals vs. trained residents)? And, what kind of vision is involved in these organizations? Do they see themselves as moving in a direction that challenges aspects of the dominant social structure? These are the questions that will be explored in relation to the case studies that follow.

ALTERNATIVE SERVICE ORGANIZATIONS (ASO)

A Definition

The diversity of ASOs makes a single definition difficult. In Montréal, those organizations developed through the efforts of diverse groups: alliances of progressive or radical professionals; dissatisfied clients of traditional state agencies; local residents organizing services for the elderly; women who have suffered rape and domestic violence; activists organizing in working class neighbourhoods lacking in health services; youth; and ex-psychiatric patients. All of these efforts encouraged clients and/or community representatives to play an active role in controlling the organization. It is not simply that a service is provided, but it must be linked to a definition of the client and/or community as an active agent in the formation and development of that service. Powell provides a useful definition, stating that ASOs are "founded by local initiative to offer an alternative to establish human services which the initiators...believe to be inadequate" (Powell 1986: 57). He argues that these organizations develop their alternative nature in contrast to government agencies because they provide a different product, such as shelter for battered women, or a different means of services, such as a drop-in centre for the ex-psychiatric, or because they reach a population that does not have easy access to existing social or health services such as the gay community. In addition, ASOs play three vital roles: they fill gaps in service delivery; develop service innovations; and advocate for social change on behalf of the groups they serve (*op. cit.*, 1986: 57-58). The organizations, although committed first and foremost to service delivery, are innovative, and link demands for social change to the service goals. Although the government will at times provide similar programs and services, it will do so *after* the initiatives have taken place in the community, and *without* the advocacy stance of the ASOs. Particularly in Québec, this pattern of community initiative, followed by government cooptation, distortion, and/or duplication on a larger scale has repeated itself in many service areas.

Stages of Development

Bassoff (1982) describes the stages of development of ASOs and argues that these stages are responses to the pressures of government and other funding. The first period, described as the "free clinic", is mostly engaged in the pursuit of social change. In this phase the ASO relies on volunteers as staff, and has a minimal amount of organizational formality. Links to outside social movements are closest and the integration of service delivery and politics are strongest. As well, an anti-bureaucratic ethos prevails, and the processes in the ASO tend to be informal. The second phase is transitional. It is characterized by increased organizational accountability and record keeping. Volunteers are drawn from pre-professional students, but the ASO still retains a commitment to its original ideology through its core leadership and the use of volunteers in service delivery. In the third and final phase, the ASO begins to utilize more traditional forms of fiscal and managerial accountability with services provided by trained professionals. However, the service remains committed to meeting the needs of the original client group.

Morgan (1981) argues that alternative agencies go through three basic changes—bureaucratization, individualization of problems by reducing a collective approach, and the professionalization of staff—which contribute to its "cooptation" by the State. These phases or stages of development are a reflection of the power of outside forces, particularly funding bodies, to define and to shape the way an ASO operates, but these pressures are not the only factor that determines the outcome. The ASO itself responds to the demands of funders, and can oppose or modify some of the funding demands. The evolution of an ASO reflects a contradiction: the more successful an organization becomes in raising outside money, the more it is pushed in a direction of political and/or social compromise. In the examples that follow, these tensions and transformations will be noted, but the continued ability to articulate oppositional ideologies, to practice alternative forms of organization, to engage in political opposition, is impressive given the pressures from funders to contain their activity.

ASOs—Québec Cases

The following information is based on a series of case studies carried out on ASOs in the Montréal area over several years at the School of Social Work, McGill University (Shragge and Letourneau, 1987). Rather than review each of the case studies, the questions about, and characteristics of, ASOs raised earlier will be addressed with specific references to them. The cases selected here are agencies that have succeeded in two respects. First, they have been able to secure funding (often inadequate given the demands for service experienced by these groups) from government or private sources that has allowed some stability for at least a period of several years. Second, they have protected certain alternative characteristics that has either differentiated them from, or have put them in, direct opposition to government agencies and departments. There are many agencies that were founded in the same periods as those in the case studies that either disappeared because of lack of funding or were absorbed into state services and agencies. Thus, the sample is not random, but will be used to try to understand the characteristics, structures and dynamics of ASOs that have survived, and ask whether, or to what extent, they are in practice, 'alternatives'.

The case studies were carried out on two community medical clinics: Clinique Pointe St.Charles, and La Clinique des Citoyens(nnes) de St.Jacques—two agencies either founded for or currently working with youth, Head and Hands, and AMCAL (A Ma Baie Citizens Action League, West Island Youth Protection), and, a rape crisis centre, CAPAS

(Centre d'Aide et de Prevention d'Assauts Sexuels de Chateauguay). In addition, two other alternatives will be cited as examples—Project Change, that works with the elderly, and Project PAL, that serves psychiatric patients. In each of the ASOs mentioned, there was little or no services for the population or the problem they were addressing when they were founded. Head and Hands was established to work with the problems of 'street people' in the sixties, and the two clinics, Pointe St. Charles and St. Jacques, provided health care to two of the poorest neighbourhoods in Montréal in the years prior to both public health insurance and government community clinics (CLSCs). Provision of service to those whose needs could not be addressed by state and private agencies was central in the origin of these agencies and continues to play an important role in their self-definition.

In the means of provision, and in their approach to service delivery, the ASOs have brought innovations. These include an emphasis on informality, to encourage accessibility, by breaking down the barriers between those giving and those receiving services. Non-professionals have been employed as front line workers. In several instances it has been the policy of the agency to employ local residents and train them as health workers. The use of volunteers and the attempt to build an environment based on mutuality and solidarity were a response to the formality and professionalism of the state agencies and hospitals. As well, all ASOs described, advocate for the needs of the group they serve. This might be expressed through attempting to organize and to mobilize the population to act on its own behalf. PAL, the Pointe Clinic, Project Change, CAPAS have all been involved in mobilizing their membership and/or clients to oppose government policies that would negatively affect their lives. These and other groups have participated in coalitions on behalf of their members or clients to oppose various government policies and actions.

The ASOs grew out of the local community, but although local residents or 'clients' do play important roles in the development of these agencies, in all the cases, there were young professionals, or students in professional training (social work, medicine), or individual community workers often employed by state agencies, who played the role of catalysts in their forming. The initial steps involve organizing local residents or potential users who eventually take control, and participate, in the development of the service. The role of professionals and organizers from the beginning is important to note because as the ASO develops, if the role and power of the professional becomes more pronounced, a tension emerges between their role and power and the principles of community control/participation. In order to mitigate these tensions, democratic structures were established that allowed the representatives of the community, or services users, to control the ASO. The context of their emergence allowed democratic structures to form more easily. The organizations studied developed within a period of community activism in Québec from the late sixties and early seventies. Subsequently, services were initiated by the women's movement. These movements contributed to the strength of the ASOs in this early period through the political critique and analysis, and the solidarity, that expressed itself in the availability of volunteer workers drawn from the community and/or the client population. The earlier experiences of the ASOs were similar to that described by Bassoff in the first phase of development. The mixture of social change activities and social or health services, coupled with volunteers' involvement gave these organizations their 'radical' style and their base of community support.

The period from the mid seventies in Québec was a contradictory one characterized by both a growth and a stability in the ASOs, and by a continued uncertainty due to changing government policies and orientations. The Castonguay reforms brought rapid expansion and growth to the health and social service sector; however, the government's policy of developing community-based CLSCs posed a threat to the many newly formed popular clinics (Lesemann 1984). Duplication of service was an issue for the State and some analysts (Godbout 1983) have argued that the use of a community clinic model was a strategy of cooptation of local leadership onto boards and swallowing up total clinics. Clinics, such as the Pointe St. Charles Clinic because of the strength of its base in the local community coupled with a clear alternative vision, were able to withstand government pressure and maintain their autonomy and ultimately negotiate a special status in their relationship with the State. Clinique St.Jacques was able to hold out for a few years, but recently has merged with a newly created CLSC and has disappeared as an independent unit. After the Castonguay reforms, the development of CLSCs forced ASOs to define a specific service mandate that did not overlap the more general programs of the local CLSC, otherwise they had to resist the implementation of the CLSC. The period of state expansion was difficult for ASOs as they represented a parallel movement to the centralized, technocratic organizations developed by the Québec State. The consequence was that many alternative organizations disappeared, partly as a result of state cooptation, and partly as a result of the declining social movements which left these organizations isolated and politically vulnerable.

The ASOs that survived this period faced a different situation during the period of cutbacks of state spending and privatization of services beginning in the late seventies and continuing until the present. State policy attempted to use community-based services as a less expensive option to the expansion of the state sector. This has put ASOs once again in a difficult position. Funding on a limited basis, and increased legitimation for ASOs has resulted, but within a specific service mandate, restricting the autonomy of the group and threatening, in the longer term, to draw these organizations into an unequal partnership in which the ASO will become an extension of state programs, while at the same time, remaining underfunded and without long-term guarantees for support. These are the issues faced by the ASOs currently. The results will not be clear for a while because policies and practices formed by the relations between these organizations and the State are in process of negotiation. The outcome, on the issue of ASO autonomy and their role as organizations involved in social change activity, will be influenced by the ability of the ASOs to organize and to mobilize both local communities and similar organizations.

Returning to Bassoff's phases of development, the ASOs examined have all moved beyond the first phase and are characterized by either the second or third phases. Receiving state and private funding has imposed a structure of management and accountability on the organizations. As well, direct service and their day-to-day operation is provided or managed by a group of paid staff. Although some of the staff may not have formal university training or its equivalent, their role in the agency is often similar to that of those who have received formal professional training. The professionals employed in the ASOs have a different orientation than others with similar backgrounds. They are committed to the ASOs and work for lower wages than they would receive in the state sector.

The Pointe St.Charles community clinic is most developed compared to the other ASOs studied. It would be identified as being in Bassoff's third phase with its unionized staff, formal management, structure, and large variety of programs. The other groups studied have remained relatively small, with a few paid staff, and a variety of funding arrangements—some more permanent than others. Volunteers are still used either to supplement service delivery or as community representatives on boards and committees. Given government funding policies, it is unlikely that these ASOs expand in the near future. At best their position will be consolidated and stabilized. Will the characteristics that led to the classification of these agencies as alternative continue, or will they follow in the directions of cooptation suggested by Morgan and end up with bureaucratic structures, with professionalized services, and little collective action? This question will be explored through examining how these organizations differ from state agencies at the level of their program, approach, and activities, and if and how their structures are democratic.

ASOs in Practice: How Alternative *is* Alternative?

The program and activities of the ASOs examined are primarily service-oriented. The service orientation as a priority, represents a shift from the earlier, and broader, approaches that the ASOs had as part of their orientation which included preventive programs, education, community action and mobilization of clients and residents. Funding sources have defined priorities as the provision of a service on an individual basis. This leads to a situation in which few resources are available for other forms of intervention. The services, however, are not duplications of those controlled by the government. Because of the small size of most of the ASOs, and the lack of a bureaucratic structure, the style of service delivery is informal, and encourages accessibility; the ASO is presented as a place to which all clients are welcome. The extent of services is more flexible, innovative, and wider ranging than state agencies. The ASOs respond to changing community needs and try to build programs to respond to these needs. The small size and the direct experience with community problems makes it easier for these agencies to respond to new issues and to develop programs within the flexibility of funding. Short-term, government funded, make work, grants are used as a means of initiating new programs.

Despite the claim that funding is the determining factor that moves ASOs almost exclusively in a service direction, political dimensions and social or community action is not lost. Client advocacy is one expression of the political dimension. Some of the ASOs play an adversarial role vis-a-vis state agencies and emphasize individual and community education as a means of helping clients to have more control over their own lives. The creation of new community resources is another facet of the activities of the ASOs. This can occur through program development, or involvement with other agencies in building new community resources. At a political level there is more variation. Agencies like Project PAL, CAPAS and the Pointe St. Charles Clinic, have been actively involved in mobilizing both clients and community residents on social issues, (i.e., opposing a recent government social assistance scheme) encouraging them to participate in demonstrations and meetings opposing government policies. However, all the agencies, except the Pointe St. Charles Clinic, have few resources and staff to support these activities. This results in the more common expression of community action for their groups—that of delegating a representative of the agency to meetings and giving the weight of the agency's name to various campaigns that are thought to be in the interests of the clients served by the ASO.

The content of the ASOs program gives priority to individual services and tends to professionalize service delivery, but, at the same time, and often despite a lack of resources available for those activities, the ASOs studied do participate in community struggles and campaigns. As well, within the category of individual services, the approach is one of client advocacy. Services themselves, because of the small size and the informality of the ASO, tend to be qualitatively different from those of the State, and challenge both policies and practices of government agencies.

The underlying philosophy of the ASOs studied is that there should be some kind of collective management. There are a variety of expressions of this principle ranging from worker collectives to structured open community elections for board members. All of the agencies have a commitment to some form of community or client empowerment and worker participation in the management of the agency. The Pointe St. Charles Clinic utilizes open community meetings to elect its board members. The staff of CAPAS and Head and Hands, work on an egalitarian, collective model. The board of Project PAL is composed, in the majority, of ex-psychiatric patients, and consumers of the agency's services. Project Change uses the concept of *prise en charge* by its members and encourages volunteers to help run the service and to play an active role in its management and board. Decision-making structures, particularly at the level of policy and orientation in all of the ASOs studied, involves community representative and/or clients and agency workers in a significant way. This does not mean that they are 'perfect' democracies or that conflicts do not exist between the roles and the power of professionals and community representatives, but participative structures exist and democratic principles are the policies of the ASOs.

A conflict exists between the demands of funding bodies for a formal structured board of directors, with a designated president and officers and a formally appointed director of the agency, and the informal, more democratic style and philosophies of the ASOs. The balance between formal structures and real agency processes is difficult to manage if the goal is to maintain the democratic process within these more formal structures. The agencies discussed have, however, been successful at maintaining their various practices and utilizing the formal structures in a way that does not completely undermine the democratic processes. Size is an important factor here. It is far easier to maintain a collective structure when the number of staff and volume of client demands is relatively small. The expansion of Pointe St.Charles Clinic in recent years has led to its internal structures becoming increasingly bureaucratic. These democratic aspects of the agencies distinguish them from state agencies. Morgenbesser *et al.*, (1981) argue that if the structures and processes of the ASOs are democratic and participative, then this gives the agencies the ability to continue to support the alternatives (i.e., the content of their activities). This is one aspect that continues to play an important part in all the agencies studied.

The tension between funding and maintaining ASO autonomy is central. The literature (Hamel 1983, Schechter 1982, Ng 1988) that discusses this question reviews the many pressures that external funding sources place on organizations. Giving priority to service delivery over other forms of intervention was discussed above. It should not be surprising that government and most private funding bodies see solutions in terms of individual change or adaptation rather than in some form or another of collective action. It is part of the dominant ideology and practice that social problems are addressed at the level of the individual. As a consequence, ASOs that start out with goals that link individual service to community or social change find out that the programs aimed at wider change do not get funded.

Government and other private funding sources have an impact in several ways; they act to destabilize ASOs by guaranteeing funds on a short-term basis, for example, on an annual basis, subject to review. Some groups are able to secure slightly longer-term funding but again the guarantees are minimal. In addition, government priorities and programs shift depending on what the social problem is 'in'. This forces groups to redefine their practice priorities in order to be eligible for funding. Short-term grants, used by government for job-creation for individuals on unemployment insurance or social assistance, have made some employees available for ASOs for specific projects, but by state regulation those hired are only there for a short period of time, and turn-over of employees on these grants is demanded. These experiences coupled with the extensive paper work and bureaucratic demands of funders, have made management of grants time-consuming and destabilizing. As well, funding bodies demand that groups change their structures in order to meet their formal requirements. Evaluation by funders demands increased record keeping and a quantification of services. This implies an internal division of labour, plus the use of forms for information gathering, and moves the ASO to become more bureaucratic in its procedures. The consequence of state and/or private funding is to change the structures, internal processes and the program content of ASOs. Despite these pressures, groups have found ways to respond that allow pressure to be moderated.

Each of the case studies showed that there was at least some alternative practice. The ability to maintain some autonomy from the constraints of their funders is a result of several factors. Each of the ASOs was able to develop particular relations with funders that demonstrate that there is a balance of power involved. The ASO was able to mobilize political support for its position through either its success in providing valued services, because of its base of support in its local community, or because of its membership in an alliance of similar agencies or groups. The most clear cut example of this process occurred with the refusal of the Pointe St. Charles Clinic to become a CLSC in the early seventies, and their mobilization of broad-based community support for that position. Subsequently, the Pointe Clinic has developed a special arrangement in which it carries out CLSC services in its community, but with an independently elected board and much more autonomy for self-definition than any CLSC. Consequently, the Clinic is still part of the 'popular movement' in its community and is actively involved in many social or political struggles. In contrast, the Clinique St. Jacques was unable to negotiate a similar arrangement and was forced to merge with a new CLSC. One of the basic differences between these two clinics was that by the time Clinic St. Jacques had to confront its choices, it had lost its base of support in the community. It was not able to mobilize support for a demand that it have a similar status to that of the Pointe Clinic. When Head and Hands was faced with a new CLSC in its community, there was concern among the members of the board and staff that the agency would be forced to merge with, or lose some of its functions to, the CLSC. However, at least partially because Head and Hands is well established in the local community and has strong ties with a variety of local institutions, it was able to continue with its mandate, and the new CLSC developed other priorities of service that did not duplicate those of Head and Hands.

The other ASOs studied have all managed, in one way or another, to secure funding that is relatively stable and leaves it with at least some autonomy. Both PAL and CAPAS are members of regroupments or federations of similar groups. These have pressured the Québec government to recognize their legitimacy and provide at least minimal funding. In the last two years, there has been ongoing debates between the government and these regroupments because the government has attempted to develop policies in the areas of funding for Rape Crisis Centres and community-based services for ex-psychiatric patients. The active involvement and challenge of these regroupments have given the individual agencies much more power in protecting and defining their own services, particularly against government agencies taking over their functions. AMCAL and, at times, Project Change has used a method of contracting with a state agency for services. This has allowed funding for the agency and at least some autonomy. However, these ASOs have been vulnerable to the state agency changing its policies and/or orientation, and redefining this funding arrangement. The winter of 1990 has brought an abrupt end of this funding arrangement for AMCAL. The base of local support is a key variable in the ASO's ability to protect itself in the negotiation process.Another way that the ASOs have been able to guard its autonomy from the demands of funders has been through maintaining a funding base that is broader than only one source. Head and Hands receives funds from the provincial government, Centraide, and private donations. This diversity allows more autonomy. Overall, the argument here is that funding is a political process, and the base of local support achieved, and the building of alliances with similar groups, are crucial factors in defending the autonomy of groups.

Another crucial variable in maintaining an alternative orientation is the internal processes and the vision of the group itself. The possibilities of cooptation, because of the pressures of outside funding, are always there. Resistance to these pressures have to begin internally through an underlying consensus on the goals and the orientation of the ASO. If over time, with turnover of staff and board members, an alternative view point in practice and ideology is not strengthened, reproduced, and renewed it will be lost. The ASO will easily give in to demands of funders. Maintaining alternative characteristics, such as internal democracy, discussions and critical debates about policy, a continued re-evaluation of practice, are all necessary if the alternative orientation is going to be protected. An alternative structure in our society can not sustain itself without an ongoing process of evaluation and renewed commitment to its direction. This is even more difficult in a period in which the social movements that helped spur the founding of the ASO have disappeared. The building of 'regroupments' has been an important means of promoting and sustaining an alternative viewpoint.

ASOs—Conclusions

What conclusions can be reached about ASOs as forms of community organization practice and alternatives to the welfare State? ASOs emerged out of social movements that aimed at social change. They are one of many expressions. As social movement activities waned, ASOs became a quasi-institutionalized expression of those visions and orientations. As these agencies began to receive funding, their policies and practices were modified to accommodate, at least partially, the demands of their funders for service delivery as a major priority over other social change oriented activity. More hierarchical structures with formal divisions of labour and an increase in the use of professional staff are part of the demands of funders. In many cases, this has led to a major transformation of some of the ASOs until they have become coopted or absorbed into state agencies (i.e., Clinique St. Jacques). In the other cases examined, aspects of alternative practice are expressed both at the level of program content and organizational structures and processes. These agencies remain at least to some extent as alternatives to the state system not only because they are outside of it, but because in many respects their policies and orientations challenge state policies and provide organizational forms that are democratic and encourage active participation of clients, workers and/or community residents. In addition, several of these agencies directly engage in, or support, activities that organize, or mobilize, local residents and clients to oppose various government policies or improve their lives that may be threatened by corporate economic decisions. Thus, ASOs represent a partial alternative as described in the earlier discussion. Certainly compromises and modifications have been made over the years so that they can be eligible for state funding, but despite pressures they remain a concrete expression of some of the goals carried by the social movements out of which these organizations grew. They still act as a point of opposition in their communities for many social issues and questions.

The community-based option has shown itself to be responsible and innovative, creating new approaches and service delivery at a level that can respond directly to a range of community needs and problems. One critique of the post-war welfare State centers on its bureaucratic structure, over reliance on professionals, and the fact that planning and control of services is remote from the local community. Clearly, the ASOs are able to address these problems, and even with their chronic underfunding. In Québec, they have provided a lower cost option when compared with the public sector often because of almost non-existent management structures and relatively low wages (I am not advocating the gross underpayment of wages that exist in many ASOs). The government would like to use these community agencies as a less expensive alternative to state services, but it is difficult to control these alternatives and their oppositional orientation.

From the viewpoint of government, ASOs do not represent a means of 'rational' planning of the health and/or social services. Planning based on local, or community initiative is by definition unpredictable. Further, providing resources to groups or organizations that do not share the same orientation as the government, and at times oppose its policies, is a political risk. Decentralization of services from the top down, utilizing community resources would be the only option for government if these agencies could also be controlled. Given that they are not, the prospects of ASOs playing a central role in the health and social services, so long as they remain an alternative is remote. For community activists, feminists, the left, ASOs do provide alternative forms of practice to state welfare, and are an important political and social resource. In the longer term, in the context of requiring an alternative to the welfare State, the actual practice of community alternatives, and the beginning tendency of their forming into regroupments, is a practice form and a tradition that can be held out in opposition to the centralized state option or the corporate privatized version. However, until ASOs are available across the province, these organizations cannot claim to provide on a universal basis, and by default, government, through its CLSCs, becomes the main provider. Although the ASOs provide an alternative to state provision in many communities, within the present structures only the State can provide on a universal basis, unless, it is willing to establish structures that can bring social planning and the necessary resources to the local community so that social and health services can be planned and organized on an autonomous, decentralized basis. The success of the ASOs demonstrate the capacity of local communities to carry out these mandates. What is missing are the decentralized structures and the transfer of resources.

Community Economic Development

In recent years, Community Economic Development (CED) has emerged in Québec as a new form of community practice. The shift toward this approach was a reaction to the decrease in militancy of citizen's organizations and popular mobilization of the late seventies, the changing political and economic climate with welfare state cutbacks, and the growth of an entrepreneurial culture in Québec, encouraged by government, and private sector. Further, many working class neighbourhoods in Montréal that had formed the centre of the popular movement (Centre Sud, Pointe St.Charles, Hochelaga-Maisonneuve) of the sixties and the seventies were crushed economically by the recession of the early eighties. These neighbourhoods faced rapid deterioration with rising and permanent unemployment, factory closures, and few economic options (Favreau 1989). Many community activists were uncertain about the direction of their interventions, what kind of activity made sense, and began to ask whether or not it is possible to invest in economic projects that embodied social values that were congruent with community interests and could reconcile a profitable economy with social intervention.

In 1986, a major conference in Victoriaville (D'Amours 1986) brought together hundreds of community activists to discuss and to reflect on issues related to community action and development. One workshop discussed some of the new initiatives that had arisen in the couple of years preceding the conference. The initial CED initiatives had been strongly supported by the State, leading many to question whether or not this support would lead to a cooptation of these initiatives by the government, and whether or not these programs would be used by the government to maintain the dominant market values and practices of the economic system.

There were hard questions raised. Was it appropriate for popular groups to replace the State in the area of job creation and form alliances with the business community in this process? Would CED end up as self-management of low-wage and precarious jobs? The men at the conference tended to ask the questions that assumed virtue in the traditional role of popular groups as raising social and economic demands. It was the women who tended to be more pragmatic, arguing that CED was a new means of continuing the struggle for social justice but without naive illusions that this could be done without dealing with economic development.

The goal, they argued, is to use government programs to advance concretely an alternative economic perspective by the creation of enterprises that are socially useful, that function democratically, and collectively, that provide stable, decent jobs, and that accommodate the needs of women workers, particularly those with children.

The parameters of this debate are similar to the ones explored earlier on ASOs. Does CED, in practice represent a viable practice alternative linking economic development to social needs and community empowerment, or will CED become an extension of the government's entrepreneurial spirit and be a way for the government to promise to revitalize poor neighbourhoods through organizing capitalist initiatives under the sponsorship of local leadership?

These questions will be explored by examining four CED groups in Montréal. These organizations are relatively new, and therefore an evaluation is difficult. However, I shall look at their origins, premises and early orientations as a means of examining these practice models. Before proceeding with this examination, I will discuss definitions and approaches to CED.

Eric Shragge

CED—Definitions

CED involves a variety of assumptions and approaches. Wachtel and Chabassol (1986) state that the term CED was first used in the U.S.A. in the early seventies to describe the creation of economic organizations owned or controlled locally in urban ghettos for the purpose of strengthening their stagnant economies, and with this process, reinforcing their physical, social and political environments. In Canada, this approach, until recently, has been limited mainly to rural areas or small cities. It has its roots in the coop movement, collective enterprise, and attempts to create self-sustaining community development.

Fontan (1988) argues that CED is oriented toward local economic development by way of the organization of an institution through which many participants from inside and outside the community can participate in its economic development. MacLeod (1986) presents CED as neither a government nor a profit-oriented enterprise, but as a third sector including a variety of economic activity ranging from informal, non-monetary exchanges, to non-profit cooperatives, and community development corporations. What differentiates this approach is its orientation towards personal and community needs and the priority it accords to local considerations. In other words, it is a decentralized approach to local economic development. The Social Planning and Research Council of B.C. states that CED is:

> concerned with fostering the social, economic, and environmental well-being of communities and regions through initiatives taken by citizens, often in collaboration with their governments, that strengthen local decision-making, self-reliance, cooperative endeavour and broad participation in community affairs (cited in Lane 1988: 185).

The main concepts identified include an emphasis on the development of the local economies in a direction that democratically links economic and social needs. Non-profit as a principle is crucial, as is broad-based social collaboration, leading to a form of local development that is neither based on the private sector nor controlled by the State.

The vision of CED is wide; MacLeod argues that the large-term goal is for increased self-determination of the community. CED is a "comprehensive, multi-purpose strategy for community survival and enhancement (of) the whole range of community resources -- human, physical, organization..." (*op. cit.*, 1986: 8-9). There are two visions or sets of goals distinguished by Wachtel and Chabassol (1986). The first is the more pragmatic view of encouraging a wide range of initiatives that can generate employment opportunities, create wealth, and stabilize and revitalize depressed areas. The second position views CED as part of a new politics—one that cuts across traditional left/right divisions. Patricia Lane (1988) argues that it is a strategy of entrenching in local communities the financial and organizational elements necessary for relatively autonomous development. It encourages innovation at the level of product design and marketing, offers opportunities for workers to experiment with democracy in the workplace, and community management opportunities leading to an accountability of the enterprise to workers and/or their communities. She sees this approach as one that bridges those skills acqired by the individual.

CED has a pragmatic side. It is a process that aims to intervene in the local economy and create jobs through various forms of economic development, and to shift economic control from outside the community (i.e., private sector or state investment) to local community institutions. The process should lead to both material or economic improvement at the local level and increase, in the longer term, political and/or social power of that community.

CED in Montréal

In Montréal, the CED projects were created in working class neighbourhoods that had a strong tradition of popular organizations and self-help groups. In these neighbourhoods the recession of the early eighties had hit hard. More and more workers were pushed into unemployment or to the fringes of the economy; for women and young workers, precarious unstable jobs in the secondary sector was the only employment avaiable. In these neighbourhoods, there were several examples of successful housing and small production cooperatives (Favreau 1988). Thus, there was a combination of oppositional and organizing experience, a few cooperative experiments, and deteriorating economic conditions that showed little signs of recovery.

Eric Shragge

The first CED initiative began in Pointe St. Charles (Fontan 1988, Favreau 1988). In 1984, in light of the different problems attacking their community—including the pressures of developers, the threat of gentrification, the closing of traditional industries, and a general deterioration of living conditions—individuals from different community organizations began a process of questioning their approaches. The conclusion reached was that the services offered by their organizations were not adequate to address the issues. Job creation had to be a priority and new enterprises were required to revitalize the area. A study recommended CED as the principle means of addressing the problems. A general assembly, that created Projet Economique Pointe St.Charles (PEP) in June 1985, attracted one hundred and fifty individuals representing corporations in the private sector, and community organizations.

The initial goals included: the establishment of a plan and policy of development for the neighbourhood; the creation of new enterprises, and subsequently, the creation of jobs; and the provision of education to the local population that would increase their level of employability. During the first years of its existence, PEP has produced an urban plan for the district; arranged financial help for thirty enterprises, old and new; participated in the creation of sixty jobs, helped maintain one hundred and twenty-five others; begun the process of improving the level of employability of local residents by establishing an enterprise school, and preparing recommendations for government on this issue; launched a self-financing campaign; and has incorporated two enterprises—one that consults in community economic development, and one in computerizing accounting. It even established a collectively owned and managed business that provides home care—thirty employees. PEP emerged as a pioneer in Montréal, building on the traditions and strengths of its local organization to help form and plan the local economy and initiate new programs and enterprises. However, a shift in orientation has occurred. PEP has enlarged its target population to include the whole Southwest sector of Montréal, changed its name to Sud Ouest, and has accepted a definition of economic development in which the private sector, and government, are the major actors. Their concerns are the employability of area residents and large scale economic development that will address the poverty and unemployment in the area. Their role as a pressure group is significant, but one that is part of a wider partnership.

La Corporation de Developpement Economique du Centre Sud (CDEC Centre Sud) was formed from a community projected titled, *Mon quartier je l'ai à coeur*. In 1985, three working groups were established composed of representatives of thirty groups and organizations in the district. The Economy and Jobs Committee benefitted from the experience of PEP, and because of the extremely poor economic conditions in the district, the Parti Québécois (PQ) government financed a pilot project to set up that CED corporation. This new organization defined two policy directions: one, to develop economic policy for the area; and two, to defend the needs and interests of its residents through the revitalization of the economy of Centre-Sud. After two years, the corporation finalized its legal structure, defined its target populations as women and youth, and helped build local enterprise through aiding sixty businesses. By April of 1987, two hundred and thirty jobs were either maintained, created or projected through their efforts. They have supported a community cafe and a newspaper. They project that between 1988 and 1991 seven hundred jobs will be either created or maintained, and that a risk capital fund of ten million dollars (eight million from the private sector) will be established. They plan to generate income through creating their own industries (i.e., information and photocopying services, and a motel). A youth and enterprise competition is held each year to encourage young entrepreneurs. Cooperative links have been established with representatives of different sectors—unions, large businesses, a university—to put together different projects such as economic indicators, and an investment fund.

La Programme Action Revitalisation Hochelaga—Maisonneuve (PAR-HM) grew out of community reflection and discussion on the local economy. Because of the economic deterioration of the area, similar processes occurred in L'Office de Planification et de Développement du Québec (OPDQ), an economic development agency of the provincial government. The corporation was launched through these two initiatives with its initial goals to stimulate and to support local economic development and to develop initiatives and entrepreneurial action that could improve the quality of life of residents. Its activities include the development and implementation of an action plan for the revitalization of the economy of the east end of Montréal; the creation of an employment committee which aims to reinsert the unemployed into the labour market; and the administration of an investment budget provided by the OPDQ. After two years it has helped fifteen enterprises to create thirty jobs, and is the key player in a committee that brings together all the economic interveners in the district.

A more recent CED initiative, Centre du développement économique du Grand Plateau (CDEC-GP), was founded formally in the winter of 1988. Information from this project was gathered through my direct involvement. A two year period of discussion and exploration of the strengths and weaknesses of a CED approach was undertaken by representatives of ten community groups prior to the launching of this organization. The groups represented are those excluded from mainstream economic life—young unemployed, single-mothers, new immigrants and refugees. The organizations combined a variety of approaches to community work such as direct service, self-help, and community action. The initial processes were ones of self-education, and defining a model of economic intervention that was appropriate to the local community. The process, although time consuming, was emphasized because the groups believed that community ownership of the CED initiative, and community empowerment through CED, was a desired outcome. In other words, CED was understood as not only a means of producing jobs and economic revitalization, but as part of a process of allowing groups who are traditionally economically and politically marginal to acquire some power and control over their neighbourhood.

Two directions were determined. The first was to build CDEC-GP through a process of community education. This implied the organization of a series of workshops with staff, volunteers, or clients of member organizations. The underlying assumption was that economic initiatives would come from the base of these groups. The target population was defined as young unemployed, women, and immigrants/refugees. Those projects that were initiated by this target population, that involved cooperative structures and processes, and that would make social contributions to the community, were given priority.

Groups have begun a planning process and have discussed projects like housing renovation and community ownership of social housing, a cooperative day care centre, a cooperative ethnic bakery, and a green house that could sell fresh herbs and spices to neighbourhood restaurants. The process of education and animation have brought groups to a point of conceptualization of projects, but more important, real participation in, and understanding of, the value and impact of CED on their own organizations. The structure of CDEC-GP gives control of the organization to its founding membership, allowing real control to remain as close as possible to the grassroots of the community.

The second important direction is the establishment of a community loan fund that will be a vehicle of financial support for projects, and along with the loan fund, a network of technical support. This is a way of helping guarantee the success of community initiatives through the availability of resource groups and individuals who can work with a group before an application is submitted right through to the completion of the project. Funds for the loans have been and will be raised from government, foundations, institutions (i.e., churches and unions), and private individuals. Funds can be used both to support community initiatives, and to lever other funds from more established lending institutions. The underlying process brings together borrowers, lenders, and technical support people into the fund's management in an alliance for community development. The loan fund is structured independently from CDEC-GP, but the majority of the seats on its board of directors are reserved for representation of CDEC-GP. The combination of this loan fund and the process of community animation unites the technical and financial infrastructure with community participation and ownership of the initiative. The emphasis is on a model of empowerment and linking social needs with economic development.

Favreau (1988), in his analysis of the development of the first three CED projects in Montréal argues that they have several characteristics that distinguish them from traditional small or medium-size enterprises. First, in their origins they emerged out of popular movements and social groups sharing a common problem (i.e., those receiving social assistance or the unemployed). Second, in their objectives, they link social goals and economic development. Third, they practice a variety of non-traditional management forms such as cooperatives, non-profit organizations, and other collective forms. Fourth, in contrast to private sector business which does not have any obligation to return its surplus to the local community, surplus through CED *is*. As well, as a strategy it tries to address the major problem facing these districts—unemployment through the creation of socially useful jobs. Finally, this process of development has the potential to build a form of economic democracy and better control over neighbourhood life by residents.

Despite these common aims, all of the CEDs are not the same in practice. Favreau (1988) develops a continuum with two poles, as a means of discussing the differences between CED projects. Pole A, views CED primarily as an economic instrument. Fundamentally, CED acts to promote the local economy and to integrate those unemployed into the labour market. Pole B, understands CED as building community alternatives, contributing to social change and developing a third economic sector (co-ops etc.). This second pole, B, represents an approach that emphasizes different organizational forms (non-hierarchical); social as well as economic development; an emphasis on local developments; providing products and services that are locally useful; and favouring democratic control of economic activity by the community. He classifies the project in Hochelaga-Maisonneuve as close to Pole A; Centre Sud in between the two poles; and PEP as close to Pole B. CDEC-GP can also be located at Pole B. The shifts in PEP/RESO, described earlier, requires that its position on this continuum be moved closer to the centre. Although there is a strong commitment to its community, it has shifted its view on economic development, and now it is much more supportive to traditional forms of private investment and control. CDEC-GP still remains closer to the second pole but has not experienced some of the pressures of state funding that the other three initiatives have. Whether it can retain its alternative characteristics and, at the same time, receive large-scale state funding is an open question at this time. This diversity is an important basis for an analysis of community practice. CED, as it has developed in Montréal, and elsewhere, embodies a variety of practice and priorities. The pressures from alliances, with both government and business, push in a direction that defines economic development as developing privately owned initiatives, and evaluates successful outcome in terms of profitability and growth. Other CED groups have tried to define success in alternative terms, particularly those related to community empowerment. A discussion of the role of government to this point and its implications will now be explored.

CED and the State

The government of Québec, during the last year of the Parti Québécois mandate, played an important role in the initial funding of both the projects in Centre Sud, and in Hochelaga-Maisonneuve. As a response to the extensive unemployment in those districts, local MNAs were looking for a means of stimulating economic growth and development and found support for the new CED initiatives. Subsequently, the three corporations negotiated administrative budgets of two hundred thousand dollars for fifteen months, plus, one hundred thousand dollars for job creation from the Office de planification et developpement du Québec (OPDQ). This support was understood as a pilot project that would be evaluated before further funding was given on a case to case basis, for three years, with the government amount reduced each year as it was assumed that the CED project would generate an equivalent amount through self-financing. The grant for the first year (1987-1988) was one hundred and fifty thousand dollars, with forty thousand dollars to be raised by the organization. The second year, the amount was one hundred and twenty-five thousand dollars, with seventy thousand dollars raised by the group, and the third year, one hundred thousand dollars for each category. Despite these arrangements, the Provincial government has no clear policy about how to deal with these new initiatives.

The City of Montréal has responded in an ad hoc way while it developed its policy on CED. It has supported these initiatives with small grants, and in the case of CDEC-GP, two employees of its economic development office are actively involved in the technical support committee of the loan fund. In September of 1988, the City, and the Fonds de Solidarité du Québec, an investment fund created by the Fédérations des Travailleurs du Québec launched a job development fund, Emploi-Montréal, with a budget of three hundred and thirty seven thousand, five hundred dollars. Projects such as those created through CED can apply to this fund for loans, and support.

Led by the City of Montréal, the winter of 1990 has brought a more concerted policy toward CED. Despite material gains brought with it, the policy is one that attempts to reshape CED into traditional forms of private development, but with community organizations playing an active role. Rather than discussing the promise of Community Economic Development, the discourse has shifted to local economic development, as part of a wide economic strategy of the City of Montréal. Job development is a clear priority but without the alternative perspective discussed earlier. A partnership in local economic development is the way in which local groups will be involved, in economic planning and development. The City will support CED groups on a contracted basis. The goal of these projects is to develop employability, and give access of the unemployed to the labour market. The priority will be given to

> Les projets qui contribuent à maximiser l'utilisation que l'on fait à Montréal des programmes des gouvernements québecois et fédéral en matière de formation, de recyclage, de recherche d'emploi, de creation d'emplois et de soutien à l'entreprise seront favorisés (Ville de Montréal 1990: 28).[1]

Although the criteria are flexible, and may include workers cooperatives, the direction and orientation is toward a market driven form of economic development with community organizations playing a role in planning and labour market integration. The vision of CED as empowering community organizations to control the local economy is lost with this policy.

CED in Montréal is at a crossroads. It grew out of the popular movements of the most impoverished neighbourhoods in Montréal, and at least initially embodied a vision of a socially useful, cooperative community economics. If, however, the major base of support for CED remains government and private sector investment, then these new initiatives will quickly lose their alternative direction. In order to prevent this from happening a broader base of support, besides government and private business, is required. CEDC-GP has moved in this direction with its loan fund. This does not mean that government support at all levels and private business interests can be excluded, but that it must be part of a wider base including trade union funds, private foundations, institutional lenders, and private individuals. The concept of a broad partnership under the leadership of community organizations themselves will allow greater control to remain in the community.

Another means of resisting the consequences of government and private control is to understand both the strengths and limits of CED. It should be clear from the results of the CED organizations to date that their role in new forms and traditional job creation is in fact very limited. Compared to large-scale lay-offs like those that occurred in the east end of the City in recent years, the new jobs yielded by CED cannot compensate for these shifts in investment. Similarly, the decision by capital, supported and encouraged by any level of government, to invest in a local economy can generate far more jobs and spin-offs for the local economy than any CED project has been able to produce.

CED has to be understood in qualitatively different terms in order to begin to confront these realities. Other forms of outcome has to be measured than job creation or job training/labour market integration programs. Activists need to understand the process of CED as one that can help a community to gain some power and control over economic levers, particularly those who have been marginalized by the economic processes of capitalism. CED organizations have to begin to view the processes through which they emerge as important as outcome defined by economic measures alone. Job creation, successful economic enterprise defined by the production of surplus, must be viewed as central in order to insure the viability of each project, but this cannot be the sole vision and objective. CED is a means or a vehicle through which communities can develop an independent economic base, one that can be used to develop social options independent of both State and capital. In addition, the process of development of CED organization can bring together low income citizens and help develop a critique of existing economic arrangements with a sense of confidence that some options can be created. These are some of the change-oriented, alternative directions that CED can take, and to some extent this has occurred with some aspects of the Montréal experience. In both PEP/RESO and CDEC-GP there is an awareness that these alternative directions are a priority, but, as the experience of the ASOs showed, political strength and community support and mobilization are necessary as a means of defending these positions. In other words, CED is inherently part of a contestation of power relations, and the dominant social definitions. As these new initiatives are drawn more closely into partnership with the State, and the private sector, an independent position will be lost if the process of development of CED projects and corporations does not include the mobilization of a large number of low-income citizens—the economically and politically marginalized and their organizations. Further, a broad base of funding is required so that these new initiatives will not become extensions and administrators of government and private sector economic planning.

CED as an Alternative

To return to the questions at the beginning of the essay, what does CED offer as a form of community organization practice? In a major way it departs from both community development and social action because it attempts to establish economic alternatives, and address economic conditions in the community. This is an important step because the community organizations have become economic interventions along with government and the private sector. A new dimension to community practice is being opened, and as was argued earlier, one that can lead in traditional or alternative directions. The model of practice that is used tends to approximate the community development approach with its emphasis on drawing together in a collaborative way, representatives of divergent interests. In CED this includes community representation through many existing organizations, government, and business, with representatives from private institutions. As a means of moving the projects along and maximizing the interests that each group can provide, this is a successful method. However, not all of these groups share the same interests and values. Many of the community groups have been engaged in struggles with business and various levels of government over issues such as housing, jobs, pollution, and the availability of public resources for combatting community problems. These basic relations have not changed. The community is still relatively powerless in these relations, and as groups have experienced historically, only broad based community alliances and mobilization coupled with an independent vision can address this question of power. CED organizations face a difficult task. If they lose their independence in developing a consensus, or alliance with business and the State, their political autonomy and vision soon disappear. On the other hand, the costs of an overt adversarial position can jeopardize their opportunities for success. As it stands now, a balance is required. A model based on community mobilization, through economic and political education, coupled with a diverse funding base can allow a CED organization to build enough independence from government and the private sector to link social needs with economic development and engage in a process in which CED is linked to community empowerment.

Do CED organizations embody an alternative form of practice? It is probably too early to answer this question. The content of the programs involve both traditionally defined employment and related training as well as the establishment of cooperatives, and non-traditional business. The pressures for traditionally defined employment will increase with state and private sector involvement. In certain educational programs used by these groups, attempts have been made to link local economic development to local social needs and the empowerment of local residents to take action on their own behalf. Those aspects of CED that attempt to empower the local communities through encouraging residents to take some control of the local economy and build independent economic institutions (i.e., loan funds), certainly are part of, and can lead to, alternative forms of practice. At this stage of development, the organizations are not hierarchically structured, but neither have there been clear statements about their commitments to alternative forms of organization, such as collectives. Participation from the local community either through individuals, but mainly through local popular organizations, is the means of maintaining at least some local accountability and control. Maintaining local support will depend on whether or not the representatives of these organizations work on CED issues with their membership. CDEC-GP has moved in this direction with structured educational sessions with many of the member groups. The process of community animation, and education will play a key role in developing and maintaining participative approaches. On the whole, it is difficult to predict what direction CED will take. There will certainly be strong pressures from the State and the private sector to move it in conventional directions. On the other hand, with the traditions of struggle embodied in many of the founding organizations, it is possible that the demands for social change and alternative directions will be a strong force in their development. However, because many community organizations have defined their agendas as a partnership with the State, and with service provision, there is a reason to be skeptical about broad-based mobilization.

Conclusion

This essay has described two types of community practice in the Montréal area—ASOs and CED. The basic issue of whether or not these forms of intervention constitute an alternative practice, as described above was examined. The discussions of each leads to the conclusion that contradictory results emerge from these forms of practice. Aspects of these approaches combined a push for social/political change with the provision of a social/health service or support for local economic development. Non-hierarchical and democratic forms of organization are present in one way or another in some of the organizations discussed. Because they are small organizations, controlled and organized locally, they do, in practice, represent a decentralized form of service delivery and economic development, that is, as opposed to the highly centralized government services particularly in Québec. In pioneering new approaches, these forms of practice are flexible in responding to, and defining, community needs, as well as intervening to address them. These are strengths, and demonstrate that communities can and do develop social and health services, as well as economic alternatives in a way that is democratic and advocates for their needs.

The conflict that groups face is their need and desire to protect their autonomy, while, at the same time, relying on government and other institutions for funding. The underlying assumptions in this paper is that there is a fundamental conflict of interest between both the State or the private sector and these alternative community organizations. The clients and communities served by these organizations are from the working class, the poor, women, and other groups who are oppressed by the structures of patriarchal capitalism. The State and the private sector have a basic stake in keeping the social order more or less the way it is, using strategies ranging from limited social reform to repression, to do so. In this period, a push for greater self-reliance, and dependence on the market place and family as a way of social reproduction, prevails as the means of maintaining profitable capital accumulation. Social and political change will obviously not be priorities for the State, and radical democratic social forms will not be encouraged. Funding from these sources will not support activities aimed at social change. Despite these limits, both ASOs and, to a lesser extent, CED have linked service provision with community mobilization and support for campaigns for social reform. As well, their democratic structures embody, at least implicitly, a vision of local control, and popular participation in social and health services and direct ownership of at least part of the economy.

Expressed in more theoretical terms, the conflict is between popular organizations and the State. The State in advanced capitalist societies is the main institution of allocation or 'redistribution' in those activities that are not profitable, those related to health and social services and social development. Community organizations in Québec, where there are few options, turn to the government for support. However, funding is not only the giving of income, it is also a relationship. This relationship tends to redefine the organization or the group receiving funding. The pressures of government can distort both the content of the group's activities and its organizational structures and processes. The pressures are present and both the ASOs and the CED projects have had to respond to them. At times groups have been coopted in the sense that their more political content and democratic structures have disappeared, or they have been absorbed entirely by state structures. As we have seen in both the ASOs and CED projects, the outcome of this relationship with state funding is not only defined by the pressures of State. Groups bring both their ideologies and traditions, links with similar organizations, and other community groups to this relation, and can resist these pressures. The outcome is not pre-determined. Both the ASOs and CED projects have had some success in defending their autonomy and building their options. Groups do not receive full autonomy in the funding game but if they consciously understand the process, have a coherent belief system and practice, understand the tactical trade-offs and how to make these while preserving their vision, and have established some community alliances and a base of support, then a degree of autonomy is possible. Autonomy of these groups is never total. Some (although compared to other activities it is small) political/social change oriented activity, some democratic forms of organization, and less reliance on formally trained professionals become expressions of this autonomy when linked to a vision of social change.

As models of community organization, both ASOs and CED have strengths and weaknesses. They tend to grow out of less politicized views of social change than community action usually suggests, but they do not assume the broad collaborative, social consensus view of traditional community development approaches. Of the two, the CED groups described tend to have entered into a more collaborative approach with state organizations and private capital then the ASOs. One reason for this is, the origin of the CED projects was in the context of an economic recession and a period ideological conservatism. In order to succeed in their agenda of large-scale job creation that addresses the massive unemployment in their districts, they have had to depend on the initiatives of government and the private sector. The motor of economic development in capitalist society is still the private investment. Although this might be shaped and redirected by CED groups and government intervention, unless this is challenged, then large-scale job creation will be tied to private investment. CDEC-GP as described earlier has at this stage of development held onto another model emphasizing the links between social and economic development. Whether the large-scale state participation and funding will shift this emphasis remains to be seen. The

CED projects have offered less of an alternative in their approaches to their social organization and economic development, but they have become a voice for community interests, particularly job creation, in the process of local economic development. Because of the economic dimension with its implicit conservative agenda, profitability, growth, etc., it will be harder for the CED groups, over the longer term, to develop a social change oriented agenda with the traditional notions of economy that they have accepted. In their origins, the ASOs embodied a more critical perspective, at least partly because they began during a period of grassroots, community-based activism and in the context of social movements that were demanding basic social change. Their relation with the State has lead to a tension between these origins, and the provision of a specific, limited social or health service, and, as a consequence, moderated these more change-oriented origins. Some ASOs have been successful either at linking social-change activities with service provision or protecting their non-hierarchical, collective forms of organization. The success is by their maintaining a vision of alternative practice, and building enough of a base in the local community, or with networks of similar groups. The ASOs, using a mixed model of consensus at their base and conflict/collaboration with the State, have been partially successful in defending their autonomy and building social options. One problem that both of these approaches face is the lack of a 'mass-base' of local support. The community-action approach would emphasize this, but because all of the groups described are service-oriented, this form of support has not been mobilized over the longer term.

Finally, how does all of this actively relate to a left agenda for the welfare State? In the current period of redefinition, the government is attempting to return at least partially the responsibility for health and social services to the community, family, and/or the private sector. Faced with these attempts, community organizations have been able to advance their opportunities for funding, but at times with the prospect of having to sacrifice autonomy. As a form of community organization practice, ASOs bring both a community action and a development model together. They act as a voice for those they serve, either advocating for individual clients, or support other oppositional activities. These are not mass-based, populist organizations, but acting as a voice of opposition they are capable of mobilizing community residents and clients. Their relative stability derived from their direct service orientation has allowed this combination of activities to occur.

Decentralization is a term that has been used by many, meaning many different things. Smith (1985) distinguishes between administrative and political decentralization. The former puts services into communities without local structures and powers to make decisions. Political decentralization implies local decision-making power and accountability to the local population. The development of ASOs and, in a beginning way, CED programs is a means of local control of social and health services and parts of economic life. These organizations remain parallel to state services and the market economy. Despite their decentralizing practice, they do not have official status as decentralized institution, and therefore remain shut out of official power relations. Both ASOs and CEDs can be understood as unofficial counter-powers to the State in their local communities. Their stability is based on the fact that they are involved in social provision, and economic development, and therefore do not display the ups and downs of social movements or many protest organizations. Their role is to negotiate with, to pressure, and to represent local needs to various levels of government form the basis of this unofficial decentralization to the local community. If these organizations remain isolated, this informal process is considerably weakened.

Is it possible for these community-based organizations to begin to build local alliances that could act as a counter-political force that can begin to challenge the authority of the State from the local level? Groups submitting material to the government in the hearings for the Rochon Commission argued that state resources should be given to these local organizations on a scale whereby they could administer and provide social and/or health services on a larger scale (ROCJMM). The government does not want to relinquish its authority to the local groups. These debates reflect the growing consciousness that local practice can be a means of building local power and decentralization.

In order to move from the practice of building community and other alliances to real community empowerment, local institutions are required to bring together oppositional forces and alternative institutions at the local level, such as community councils and Tables de concertation. The organizations described in this discussion can play a central role in helping to develop these new forms of community organization. However, decentralization also requires official sanction, and a redistribution of the control of government planning and spending at the local level. This is a political process, one that demands changes in the social structures themselves, and one that provides real decision-making power in the local community. The push for neighbourhood councils at the urban level has been widely debated in Montréal, although promising greater local control and direct democracy, these, and other decentralized structures, face problems such as the consequences of their being controlled by local elites and the dangers of coopting of local representatives through a compartist structure (Panet-Raymond 1989). Unless decentralization is part of an oppositional, democratic strategy that offers an alternative vision, it is unlikely to produce either interest by the local population, or become a means of struggling for social change.

The present context presents both opportunities and dangers for ASOs and CED. The shift to a conservative agenda since the beginning of the eighties, particularly at the level of social welfare and local economic development, has created a space for local organizations as part of their vision. Local groups become part of the shift from the State to a combination of the private sector, the community, and the family as playing a more central role in social provision. The concept of partnership discussed in the introduction describes the situation in which the government is holding out a hand for groups such as ASOs to join in a redefinition of the social and health services. Similarly in CED, local organizations have become part of a process of local economic development, driven by the private sector. The consequences of the government actions are profound. They can integrate groups that have acted independently and represented community interests into either the network of state social and health services or local economic development. At the same time, state action such as cutting back services and finding less expensive alternatives (often because of cheap labour in community-based organization), becomes increasingly legitimated because of the presence and participation of these community-based organizations.

But, this context provides opportunities. The State, in a sense, *needs* these local groups if it is to carry out its programs. Just as the groups can act to legitimate state action, they have power to challenge these state policies and orientations, and in the present context there is a limited space for negotiation. Those ASOs that have organized into 'regroupments' have had an impact on state policy at the level of service delivery and funding of community-based alternatives. Groups in the alternative mental health network have had some limited successes and, at the same time, the conflict with government has made the role of alternatives more powerful in the process of policy definition. In order to move in this direction the regroupments have to play a central role, and have a clearly articulated vision of what they want, and how they are alternative. If the vision is missing then ASOs become little more than inexpensive options to a more centralized form of state provision. Similarly, CED projects from several communities, together, have been meeting with representatives from the City of Montréal. However, a clear vision of CED has not emerged, and the groups still have a range of viewpoints. With large amounts of money being invested, the push is towards a model in which community representation acts as a voice for job creation rather than a force for local control of economic life.

Both CED and ASO offer a viable and potentially alternative form of community intervention. Their orientation has been shaped both by external and internal factors. The shift in context and state social policy, from one emphasizing central control and expansion, toward the conservative agenda has shaped the development of both of these organizations. Yet, the response of these organizations is also central. Their ability to maintain clear vision, and their ability to build local community support and federate with similar organizations becomes the central factor in their ability to protect their practice, and, orientation.

NOTES

1. "Special attention will be given to projects which contribute to a better use in Montréal of provincial and federal programs related to training and upgrading information, job research and creation, and support to enterprises."

BIBLIOGRAPHY

Althusser, L. (1971) *Lenin, Philosophy and Other Essays*, London: New Left Books.

Bassoff, Betty Z. (1982) "The Community Clinics: Will They Survive?", *Social Work in Health Care*, Vol. 8 (1) Fall: pp. 71-79.

Benington, John. (1976) *Local Government Becomes Big Business*, London: Community Development Project.

Bolger, Steve; Paul Corrigan, Jan Docking, and Nick Frost. (1981) *Towards Socialist Welfare Work*, London: MacMillan Press.

Braverman, Harry. (1974) *Labor and Monopoly Capital: The Degradation of Work in the Twentieth Century*, New York: Monthly Review Press.

Brody, Hugh. (1975) *The People's Land: Eskimos and Whites in the Eastern Arctic*, Aylesbury: Penguin Books.

Brook, Eve and Ann Davis. (1985) "Women and Social Work", pp.3-27, in Eve Brook and Ann Davis (eds.), *Women, The Family and Social Work*, London: Tavistock Publications.

Carchedi, G. (1977) *On the Economic Definition of Class*, London: Routledge Direct Publications.

Carchedi, G. (1983) *Problems in Class Analysis*, London: Routledge Direct Publications.

Carniol, Ben. (1985) "Intervention with Communities", in Shankar A. Yelaja (editor), *An Introduction to Social Work Practice in Canada*, Toronto: Prentice Hall.

Castells, M. (1977) *The Urban Question*, London: Edward Arnold.

Castonguay-Nepveu, Québec (1971) "Report of the Commission of Enquiry on Health and Social Services", *Part One—Development*, Vol. iii, Tomes I & II, Québec.

Castonguay-Nepveu, Québec (1972) *Part Four—Social Services*, Vol. vii, Tomes I & II, Québec.

CIPFA (1983) *Personal Social Service Statistics 1983-84*, Statistical Information Service, London, England.

Cockburn, Cynthia. (1977) *The Local State: Management of Cities and People*, London: Pluto Press.

Cohen, Stanley. (1975) "It's Alright for You to Talk", in Roy Bailey, and Mike Brake, (eds.), *Radical Social Work*, London: Edward Arnold.

Cohen, Stanley. (1973) *Folk Devils and Moral Panics*, Great Britain: Paladin.

D'Amours, Martine. (1986) "L'économie communautaire casse-queule ou possible?", *La Vie En Rose*, decembre, pp. 21-24.

Davies, Linda. (1985) "Social Workers' Experience of Work Under Changing Administrative Forms: An Empirical and Theoretical Critique of Braverman", Ph.d. Polytechnic of North London, England.

Davies, Linda and Wendy Thomson. (1983) "The C.S.S. Malaise: A Second Opinion", *Intervention 67*.

Devon County Council, Social Service Department. (1979) *Priorities and Workloads*, Research and Training Section, Exeter, England.

Devon County Council, Social Service Department. (1982) *Report and Accounts 1982-83*, Exeter, England.

Divay, G. and J. Godbout. (1979) *La Decentralisation en Pratique*, INRS-Urbanisation, Montréal, Québec.

Favreau, Louis. (1989) "L'économie communautaire: un défi," *Relations* mars, pp. 42-46.

Favreau, Louis.(1989). *Mouvement populaire et intervention communautaire de 1969 à nos jours*, Centre formation populaire et Les Editions du Fleuve, Montréal.

Favreau, Louis. (1988). "Le développement économique communautaire en milieu urbain: nouvelle stratégie d'intervention sociale auprés des collectivités", dans Christine Corbeil(editor) *Le travail social aujourd'hui actes du congrés 1987*, RUFUTS, Montréal.

Fontan, Jean-Marc. (1988) "Le développement économique communautaire à Montréal", *Possible*, Vol. 12, No. 2, Printemps, pp. 183-195.

Foucault, M. (1975) *Discipline and Punish*, Harmondsworth: Penguin.

Foucault, M. (1980) *Power/Knowledge*, C. Gibson (ed.), Brighton: Harvester.

Freire, P. (1970) *Pedagogy of the Oppressed*, Harmondsworth: Penguin.

Frost, Nick. (1977) "Working for the State: The Determinants of the Social Work Labour Process," M.A. Thesis, University of Warwick, September.

Gamble, Andrew. (1982) *Britain in Decline*, Boston: Beacon Press.

Glastonbury, Bryan, David M. Cooper, and P. Hawkins. (1980) *Social Work in Conflict*, London: Croom Helm, 1980.

Godbout, Jacques. (1983) *La participation contre la democratie*, Les Editions Coopératives Albert Saint-Martin, Montréal.

Gordon, Linda. (1985) "Child Abuse, Gender and The Myth of Family Autonomy", *Child Welfare*, LXIV: 213-224.

Gordon, Linda. (1988) *Heroes of Their Own Lives: The Politics and History of Family Violence*, New York: Viking Press.

Gough, Ian. (1979) *The Political Economy of the Welfare State*, London: MacMillan Press.

Governement du Québec (1989). *Improving Health and Well-Being in Québec: Orientations*, Ministère de la Santé et des Services Sociaux.

Graham, Hilary. (1983) "Caring: A Labour of Love", in Janet Finch and Dulcie Groves (eds.), *A Labour of Love: Women, Work and Caring*, London: Routledge and Kegan Paul.

Great Britian, CMND. 3703 (1968) *Local Authority and Allied Personal Social Services*, HMSO, London, England.

Hall, Stuart; Charles Critcher, Tony Jefferson, John Clarke, and Brian Roberts. (1978) *Policing The Crisis: Mugging, The State and Law and Order*, London: MacMillan.

Hamel, Pierre. (1983) "Crise de la redistribution étatique et financement des organisation populaires", *Revue Internationale d'Action Communautaire*, 10, automne, pp. 65-76.

Heraud, Brian. (1978) "Professionalism and Social Work", in *Professional and Non-Professional Roles*, Great Britain: The Open University Press.

Hobsbawm, Eric. (1965) *Industry and Empire*, Hammondsworth: Penguin.

Jessop, B. (1982) *The Capitalist State: Marxist Theories and Methods*, Oxford: Martin Robertson.

Joyce, Patrick; Mike Hayes, and John William. (1985) "Public Sector Trade Unions and Democracy", Draft manuscript research report, Polytechnic of North London.

Lane, Patricia. (1988) "Community-Based Economic Development: Our Trojan Horse", *Studies in Political Economy*, Spring, No. 25.

Leonard, Peter.)1979) "In Defence of Critical Hope", *Social Work Today* 10.

Leonard, Peter. (1990) "Contesting the Welfare State in a Neo-Conservative Era: Dilemmas for the Left", *Journal of Progressive Human Services*, Vol. 1, No. 1.

Lesemann, Frederic. (1984) *Services and Circuses*, Montréal: Black Rose.

Lesemann, Frederic and Gilbert Renaud. (1980) "Loi 24 et transformations des pratiques professionnelles en service social", *Intervention* 58.

Lipsky, Micheal. (1980) *Street Level Bureaucracy*, New York: Russell Sage.

Manchester Guardian Weekly (1987) December 20.

McLeod, Greg. (1986) *New Age Business—Community Corporations that Work*, Canadian Council on Social Development, Ottawa.

Ministry of Social Affairs, Québec. (1980) *Allocations de Masses Territoire de CSS à l'Aide d'Indices de Population*, Direction générale de la planification et d'évaluation, January.

Ministry of Social Affairs, Québec. (1982) *Etat de la Situation, 31 mars 1982*, March.

Ministry of Social Affairs, Québec. (1982) *Répartition Budgétaire—Région 6A*, Direction générale des programmes de service sociales, April.

Ministry of Social Affairs, Québec. (1982) *Détail de Personnel, Etat de Situation des CSS au 31 mars*, March.

Mitchell Juliet and Ann Oakley (eds.) (1986) *What is Feminism?*, New York: Pantheon Books.

Morgan, Patricia. (1981) "From Battered Wife to Program Client: the State's Shaping of Social Problems", *Kapitalistate*, (9): 17-39.

Morgenbesser, Mel, Susan Notkin, Nancy McCall, Bart Grossman, and Elizabeth Nachreiner-Cory (1981) "The Evolution of Three Alternative Social Service Agencies", *Catalyst*, No. 11, pp. 70-83.

Ng, Roxana. (1988) *The Politics of Community Services: Immigrant Women, Class and the State*, Toronto: Garamond.

Panet-Raymond, Jean. (1989) "The Future of Community Groups in Québec, The Difficult Balance Between Autonomy and Partnership with the State", *Canadian Social Work Review*, Vol. 6, No. 1, Winter, pp. 126-135.

Panet-Raymond, Jean. (1989) "La démocratie et la décentralisation à Montréal", *Nouvelles Practiques Sociales*, Vol. 2, No. 2, pp. 175-177.

Packman, Jean. (1981) *The Child's Generation: Child Care Policy in Britain*, 2nd edition, Oxford: Basil Blackwell and Martin Robertson.

Paine, Robert. (1977) "The nursery game: colonizer and colonized in the Canadian Arctic", in Robert Paine, (ed.), *The White Arctic: Anthropological Essays in Tutelage and Ethnicity*, St. John's: Memorial University.

Parsloe, Phyllida and Olive Stevenson. (1978) *Social Service Teams: The Practitioners View*, Great Britain: Department of Health and Social Security.

Parton, Nigel. (1979) "The National History of Child Abuse: A Study in Social Problem Definition", *British Journal of Social Work*, 9: 431-451.

Parton, Nigel. (1981) "Child Abuse, Social Anxiety and Welfare", *British Journal of Social Work* 11: 391-414.

Parton, Nigel. (1985) *The Politics of Child Abuse*, London: MacMillan.

Phillipson, C. and Walker, A. (eds.) (1986) *Ageing and Social Policy*, Aldershot: Gower.

Poulantzas, N. (1978a) *Political Power and Social Classes*, London: Verso.

Poulantzas, N. (1978b) *Classes in Contemporary Capitalism*, London: Verso.

Poulantzas, N. (1980) *State, Power, Socialism*, London: Verso.

Powell, David M. (1986) "Managing Organizational Problems in Alternative Service Organizations", *Administration in Social Work*, Vol. 10(3), Fall, pp. 56-62.

Rees, Stuart. (1978) *Social Work Face to Face*, New York: Columbia University Press.

Regroupements des Organismes Communautaires Jeunesse du Montréal Métropolitain(ROCJMM). (1986) *Le développement des orgnismes communautaires jeunesse: une nécessite-document de reflexion*.

Renaud, M. (1984) "New Middle Classes in Search of Hegemony", from A. Gagnon (ed.), *Québec State and Society*, Toronto: Metheun.

Roderick, R. (1986) *Habermas and the Foundations of Critical Theory*, London: Macmillan.

Rojek, C., Peacock, C. and Collins, S. (1988) *Social Work and Received Ideas*, London: Routledge.

Satyamurti, Carole. (1979) "Care and Control in Local Authority Social Work", pp.89-103, in Noel Parry, Mike Rustin and Carole Satyamurti (eds.), *Social Work, Welfare and the State*, London: Edward Arnold.

Saunders, P. (1981) *Social Theory and the Urban Question*, London: Hutchinson.

Schechter, Susan. (1982) *Women and Male Violence—the Visions and Struggles of the Battered Women's Movement*, Boston: South End Press.

Simpkin, Mike. (1979) *Trapped With Welfare*, London: MacMillan.

Shearer, Ann. (1979) "Tragedies Revisited", *Social Work Today*, January 9, 16:23.

Smith, B.C. (1985) *Decentralization: The Territorial Dimension of the State*, London: George Allen and Unwin.

Spencer, Claudine. (1973) "Support as a key problem in social work", *Social Work Today*, 3: 4-7.

Stedman-Jones, Gareth. (1977) "Class Expression vs. Social Control: A Critique of Recent Trends in The Social History of Leisure", *History Workshop*, 4.

Thomson, W. (1988) *Trying to Make Welfare Work*, Ph.D. Thesis, Department of Social Administration, University of Bristol, England.

Tudiver, Neil. (1982) "Business Ideology and Management in Social Work: The Limits of Cost Control", *Catalyst* 13.

Vaillancourt, Y. (1983) "Le Parti Québecois et le social", Unpublished paper, Université de Montréal, Montréal.

Ville de Montréal (1990) *Partenaires dans le développement économique des quartiers*.

Voigt, Louise. (1986) "Welfare Women", pp. 80-92, in Helen Marchant and Betsy Wearing (eds.), *Gender Reclaimed*, Sydney: Hale and Iremonger.

Walker, Alan. (1984) Book Review, *New Socialist*, 16 (March-April): 50-51.

Wilson, Elizabeth. (1977) *Women and the Welfare State*, London: Tavistock.

COMMUNITY ACTION
Organising for Social Change
by Henri Lamoureux, Robert Mayer, and Jean Panet-Raymond
translated by Phyllis Aronoff and Howard Scott

...*thoroughly readable and immensely useful work...displays the remarkable depth of experience the authors gained through their work...Community Action traces the recent developments within Québec's nascent social-activist community. The authors chronicle the successes and failures of various popular movements...an immensely pragmatic work and one that will no doubt become required reading for community activists throughout North America and Europe.*
Quill and Quire

...*a capable historical overview of community action...*
Ottawa Citizen

190 pages
Paperback ISBN: 0-921689-20-9 $16.95
Hardcover ISBN: 0-921689-21-7 $35.95

Fighting For Hope
Organizing to Realize Our Dreams
by Joan Newman Kuyek

Starting from the experience of ordinary people, the author looks at how 'scientific management', in the form of political systems, educational systems, and communication systems, all work to diminish the power and the ability of Canadians to determine their own futures.

225 pages
Paperback ISBN: 0-921689-86-1 $16.95
Hardcover ISBN: 0-921689-87-X $35.95

BLACK ROSE BOOKS
has published the following books of interest

Rita Arditti, Pat Brennan, and Steve Cavrak, Science and Liberation
Christian Bay and Charles C. Walker, Civil Disobedience
Micheline Beaudry, Battered Women
Etienne de la Boétie, The Politics of Obedience
Murray Bookchin, The Limits of the City, *2nd edition*
Steve Butterfield, Amway:The Cult of Free Enterprise
Noam Chomsky, Radical Priorities
Claire Culhane, Still Barred From Prison
Chris DeBresson, Understanding Technological Change
Deborah Harrison, The Limits of Liberalism:The Making of Canadian Sociology
Gary Kinsman, The Regulation of Desire: Sexuality in Canada
Joan Newman Kuyek, Fighting For Hope: Organizing to Realize Our Dreams
Frédéric Lesemann, Services and Circuses:Community and the Welfare State
William R. McKercher, Freedom and Authority
Cindy Patton, Sex and Germs: The Politics of Aids
Fran Peavy with Myra Levy and Charles Varon, Heart Politics
Marc Raboy and Peter A. Bruck, eds., Communication: For and Against Democracy
Diana Ralph, Work and Madness:The Rise of Community Psychiatry
Dimitrios Roussopoulos, ed., The City and Radical Social Change
Dimitrios Roussopoulos, Green Politics

send for our our free complete catalogue of books
BLACK ROSE BOOKS
P.O.Box 1258 Succ. Place Du Parc
Montréal, Québec H2W 2R3 Canada

Printed by the workers of
Les Editions Marquis, Montmagny Québec
for
BLACK ROSE BOOKS LTD.